Dr Mavor and Mr Bridie

DR MAVOR AND MR BRIDIE

Memories of James Bridie

RONALD MAVOR

CANONGATE
and
THE NATIONAL LIBRARY OF SCOTLAND

First published in 1988 by **Canongate
Publishing Limited**, 17 Jeffrey Street,
Edinburgh EH1 1DR,
and **The National Library of Scotland**,
George IV Bridge, Edinburgh EH1 1EW

Text © 1988 Ronald Mavor

The Publishers acknowledge subsidy
of the Scottish Arts Council
towards the publication of this volume.

British Library Cataloguing in Publication Data
Mavor, Ronald
    Dr Mavor and Mr Bridie: memories of James Bridie.
    1. Drama in English. Bridie, James, 1888-1951
    I. Title
    822'.912

ISBN 0-86241-198-X

Reproduced from disc by Polyprint, 48 Pleasance, Edinburgh

Printed and bound by Bell and Bain Limited,
Thornliebank, Glasgow

For James, Ingrid, and Amy Bridie Mavor.

Author's Note

Scottish writing has been haunted by the divided personality. From Hogg's *Confessions of a Justified Sinner*, through *Dr Jekyll and Mr Hyde*, up to R. D. Laing's *The Divided Self*, the Scot has shown an obsession with what Gregory Smith, in 1919, called 'the Caledonian antisyzygy', meaning an attempt to unite opposites. I suspect that it has as much to do with the geography as with the history of the country.

My father, who was Dr Mavor and Mr Bridie, returned from a really hard and nasty war (Ypres, the Somme, and Persia) to general practice in Langside, Glasgow. But he was an artist, and his passion was the theatre — then, in Scotland, very much in its infancy. He became a major playwright, the legitimate successor to Shaw, writing plays which were, and are, performed furth of Scotland and, as writer and entrepreneur, laid the foundations for Scotland's current lively theatrical scene.

In his autobiography, *One Way of Living*, written half way through his career as a dramatist, he presented himself as a 'happy bourgeois literary man' who paid his bills, did not beat his wife, and was at peace with the world. I don't believe that Dr Mavor and Mr Bridie lived quite so happily together.

This book is, in some sense, a complement and a corrective to *One Way of Living*. What my father dealt with at length (his school and university days) I have skipped over; what he omitted (the First World War and most of his writing career) I have attempted to fill in. Moreover, by giving space to a number of his drawings and paintings, I have shown something of his little-known skill as a graphic artist. As his child, I have adopted some of his mannerisms — initial capitals and unattributed names and the odd archaism. I like them, and the publishers have generously connived at them.

A debt of gratitude is due to my mother, Rona Mavor, who collected, shortly after my father's death in 1951, most of the letters which I quote, and to their owners who sent them to her to be transcribed. Especial thanks are due to Mrs Naomi Sim, the Baroness Elliot of Harwood, Dr Ian Glen and the Trustee of the late Sir Tyrone Guthrie.

I

'James Bridie' was the name which Dr Osborne Mavor adopted when he became a writer. The Mavors were in many ways an archetypal Scottish family, moving from the rural north and establishing themselves in the prosperous West End of Glasgow in the late nineteenth century. They brought with them a simple piety, a commitment to the Protestant work ethic and a taste for the respectable pleasures enjoyed by the new bourgeoisie of the time. Osborne Mavor's choice of pseudonym, taken from his grandfather and a great-grandfather, reflects a sense of this family; and, indeed, its ideas and its values, for better or for worse, made him the writer he became. I hope, therefore, that the reader will bear with me if I spend a few pages retracing the history of one of these remarkable families.

New Aberdour in the district of Buchan, in the north-easterly corner of Aberdeenshire, was, in the first half of the nineteenth century, a self-contained community, probably little changed in several hundred years. Each villager occupied a lot consisting of a house and garden, four unenclosed fields or riggs, and a share of the common grazing land. Those who were also craftsmen made their shoes, suits, harness, cupboards or coffins to order when required and were paid more often in barter than in money. There were two 'merchants' who operated a modest trade between the village and Fraserburgh or Aberdeen, taking animals to the market and bringing back tea, sugar, salt and the finer cloths. Itinerant vendors of fish or ribbons brought to the village news of the wider world.

James Mavor was born there, to the maker of shoes, in 1828. He went to the University in Glasgow. The University still observes a mid-term holiday called 'Meal Monday'. It was instituted so that students from the country and the Highlands could go home for another sack of oatmeal, the staple of their diet in the land of porridge.

Not long before he moved south a remarkable event in the history of Scotland had happened. Thomas Chalmers, in 1843, had led 451 ministers out of the General Assembly of the Church of Scotland — its annual parliament — to found the Free Church. The argument had been essentially about whether the Kirk should be 'the uncontrolled mistress of her own doings' and recognise no head but God, as the seceders believed, or whether the Law of the Land was paramount. Those who left the established Church walked out of their churches and their manses and relinquished their stipends. It was a courageous act. As most of the schools in the country pertained to the Church of Scotland, the new Free Church set about founding its own schools.

This was very recent history, and still a burning topic of discussion, when James Mavor, at the age of twenty-two, married and took charge of a Free Church school in Stranraer in 1850. His wife, Mary Ann Bridie, was the daughter of a sea captain, plying in sail to Russia and to China from Dundee. Captain Bridie used to bring back exotic gifts, once a monkey and once an ostrich which, it is related, swallowed his wife's knitting, needles and all.

The curriculum of Mr Mavor's school consisted very largely of Latin and the Shorter Catechism. The standard punishment was the learning of psalms or chapters of Isaiah, supplemented in severe cases by the tawse. Stranraer was a quiet country town and, one may speculate, probably not, in spite of its wider range of social contacts, disturbingly different from New Aberdour. There the Mavors began what was to become a properly numerous and remarkable Victorian family. There were eleven of them, of whom eight survived. James, junior, was to become a Professor of Economic History in Toronto and a friend of Tolstoy, William Morris and Kropotkin. Harry and Sam became engineers and sailed the seven seas, Sam for a spell as an officer in the Japanese navy. Alfred made and lost fortunes and died in a doss house with, it is said, the invention of a dial telephone in a worn attaché-case under his bed. Ivan was killed when a Russian ship blew up in St Petersburg harbour. Isabella became a missionary in India. Nan and Jessie lived to a good age, unmarried, devoted to good works and proper behaviour.

In 1862 the young family moved to Glasgow. Mr Mavor was appointed to a school associated with the Free St Matthew's Church in the West End of that then burgeoning and probably alarming city.

Professor James Mavor, the son who went to Toronto, wrote in his My Windows on the Street of the World:

The change from the semi-rural and compact society of a country town to a city crowded with an industrial population highly diversified and very individualistic was at first rather depressing. In the country everyone knew everyone else. Everyone had a recognised place in the community. In the town no one knew, or cared to know, his next door neighbour. In the country there was little ostentatious display of wealth, little subservience to it; definite obligations attached to its possession. There are rural districts where the people have become lackeys, but these cannot be held to represent the country as a whole. The sordid peasant is not unknown, but even in his case sordidness is not regarded by his neighbours as a virtue, and it is restricted by a sense of the advisability of keeping on good terms with the community. Over all there is the saving grace of rustic humour. In the town vulgar display abounds; there is much wealth and poverty. Sense of obligation on the ground of social position has little force, commercial keenness is looked upon with approval; and while there is abundance of caustic wit, there is, in general, slender humour. These reflections have been given a general application; but they may be regarded as being especially applicable on the one hand to the country districts of Aberdeenshire and Wigtonshire, and on the other to Glasgow, the commercial and industrial capital of Scotland.

Not long before, in 1840, the Chief Constable of Glasgow had written:

In the very centre of the city there is an accumulated mass of squalid wretchedness unequalled in any other town in the British dominions. Here there is concentrated everything that is wretched, loathsome, dissolute and pestilential. These places are filled by a population of many thousands of miserable creatures. The houses are unfit even for styes, and every apartment is filled with a promiscuous crowd of men, women and children, all in the most revolting state of filth and squalor. In many of the houses there is scarcely any ventilation and,

3

from the extremely defective sewerage, filth of every kind constantly accumulates.

The population of the city had risen from 83,000 at the beginning of the century to 345,000 in 1851.

The congregation of Free St Matthew's Church, however, were fairly well to windward of all this, and although Glasgow has retained many of its social and public health problems even to the present day it was then on the verge of great prosperity. The 1860s and 70s were a boom time for shipbuilding and many fortunes were made in Glasgow. Harry Mavor started a modest electrical engineering business in the first days of electricity and provided arc lights for Queen Victoria's evening Review at Holyrood Palace in Edinburgh in 1881. The plant consisted of a small steam engine which drove three dynamos, each of which fed an arc light. Sam marched past in the parade and then rushed back to the little wooden hut in the Palace grounds and stoked the boilers. Being somewhat inexperienced he opened a valve too quickly and sent a steaming mixture of water and soot up the chimney and over many of the spectators. Harry was twenty-three and Sam eighteen. It must have been exciting for them.

I did not know Harry, my grandfather, but I knew Sam in his later years. He was an extremely dapper little man with a white French beard, a velvet smoking jacket and cap. He looked comfortable and everything in the house which he shared with his three sisters was of the best: French carpets, Louis XV furniture and a grand piano specially designed in that style by Whytock & Reid of Edinburgh.

The full panoply of their establishment in Crown Gardens was unfurled for the Aunts' Christmas Dinner. All the family were required to attend and the house was full of uncles, aunts and cousins, all in their best. The last such party must have been in 1938 because I remember that we were living in Drymen, some seventeen miles north of Glasgow, and spent the night in the Queen Street Station Hotel. There was a blazing coal fire in the bedroom.

The smaller children sat at a couple of little tables and had, I suspect, more uninhibited fun than the large party round Uncle Sam's grand mahogany table, but everyone ate their way through a dinner from which no possible trimming was omitted and silver candlesticks and starched linen provided the ground bass for the white ties and boiled shirts of the gentlemen, the evening dresses and jewellery of the ladies, the black gingham and lace of the servants.

After dinner one was expected to recite — Tennyson for preference — but that year I think we were reprieved as Uncle Jack had brought a cinematograph film of a holiday on his yacht. I don't remember anyone singing or playing the piano, although Aunt Jessie had some reputation as a singer of drawing-room ballads when younger. The piano, under a large Japanese painting, was covered with a Paisley shawl and a score of photographs of 'very dear friends of the family', among them Elizabeth and Albert, later George VI. I have heard that a musician, invited to play, once insisted on opening the lid of the grand piano. Janet, the housemaid, was sent for, dust-sheets brought, the photographs carefully stacked, the shawl removed, the lid, after some exploratory fiddling about, opened and, at the first chord, a cloud of dust, several bats, and a small owl flew out and astonished the gathering.

When the Mavor Aunts had all finally been received into that Higher Drawing Room to which they had aspired, their doings, observed or imagined, provided a treasure house of anecdotes for the next generation which, I suspect, survives undiminished among the diaspora of Mavor descendants in Canada.

James Mavor, the Free Church schoolteacher from New Aberdour, who begat these and his other far-faring children, died in 1879 at the age of fifty-one, having spent less than a score of years in Glasgow. His wife, the daughter of Captain John Bridie of Dundee, lived another seventeen years and died in 1896. By then Harry and Sam Mavor had 'made good' and James, junior, was a Professor in Toronto. Of the large family it was Professor James Mavor, the oldest, who most valued, for all his extensive international acquaintance, the tap root that bound him to the recently still mediaeval life of New Aberdour. He had visited there for twenty years. The younger members of the family valued it less. The Aunts were, I think, rather ashamed of it. A family was emancipating itself and moving into a new world. It was happy to drive its plough over the bones of its ancestors.

The next generation had, through James, its widest flowering in Canada. In Scotland, the bachelor Sam and his sisters left no issue. The son of the Ivan who was killed in the Russian explosion became a minister in the Episcopal Church and retired, unmarried, to the Highlands of his mother's people. Harry Mavor married and had

Harry Mavor, James Bridie's father, by Maurice Greiffenhagen.

three sons, two of whom continued in the family business, Mavor & Coulson Ltd.

The eldest of the three sons, Osborne Henry Mavor, became a physician and then a writer of stage plays. When it seemed expedient to disguise this double personality he called himself James after his grandfather, the Free Church schoolteacher, and Bridie after his grandmother's father, the sea captain from Dundee.

2

I have portraits of Harry Mavor and of his wife Janet Osborne, my grandparents. The portrait of Harry Mavor is by Maurice Greiffenhagen who was Head of Painting at the Glasgow School of Art. It is a most sensitive portrait of a man with copper-coloured hair, going a little grey. He has deep-set, tender, blue eyes, a full moustache and a short beard. The cheek-bones are high and prominent, like Maxim Gorky. The man looks intelligent and delicate. Harry Mavor was both these things.

His wife, painted by Bessie McNicol, has an heroic carriage. Dressed in black, with a high collar, her magnificent head and gentle, grey eyes are unmistakably true to what one knows of her character. She was the oldest of a large family of girls, left fatherless when quite young. She was profoundly religious and expended her concern for her siblings into a wider and wider circle of generous activity. Finding herself married to a born rationalist — for it was not long after the publication of Darwin's *Origin of Species*, a bomb placed under mid-nineteenth-century evangelism, that they married — one guesses that her confidence was much tried but she wrote godly letters to her son right through the 1914-18 War and her portrait is that of someone who is assured of certain certainties. The Mavors compromised by worshipping at the church of a lively and forward-looking minister, and, by all accounts, lived happily together for thirty years.

I never knew my grandmother, but her younger sisters Nancy and Edie were little bundles of energy and intelligence. When I was an ailing medical student I was sent down to Kilcreggan, on the Firth of Clyde, for a week or two and the two grey-haired, bespectacled ladies filled me with fun and liveliness. Aunt May, who had married

Janet Osborne Mavor, James Bridie's mother, by Bessie McNicol.

a missionary, was more solemn. But the Osborne Aunts, as opposed to the Mavor Aunts, were innocent of the respectable aspirations of the new bourgeoisie of rising Glasgow. The Osbornes came from Ayrshire of dairy-farming stock. The father farmed a piece of land on which Burns wrote 'Man Was Made To Mourn'. They inherited Burns in a livelier mood.

Harry Mavor married Janet Osborne in the Pollokshields Free Church in 1886. Four years before, Harry Mavor had been a medical student but a financial difficulty had led him to give up the study of Medicine and become an engineer with, as has been said, a particular interest in the new electric lighting. He prospered only moderately. For some years the Mavors lived in the country, in East Kilbride, then in Dennistoun in the east end of Glasgow, and then in Windsor Circus, just west of the Botanic Gardens in Kirklee.

My father, the future playwright, was born on January 3rd 1888. He has described his early years and schooldays in his autobiography, *One Way of Living*. These stories of the Glasgow Academy and the Masters of his day populated my own early childhood. He told, and told in his autobiography, few tales of life in the Mavor home. His father, and his uncle James, were friends of the remarkable school of painters known as the Glasgow Boys. James edited a magazine called *The Scottish Art Review* for a brief period. Harry Mavor's house was decorated in the Arts and Crafts style whose simplicity and lack of ostentation appealed, one may guess, to his wife as much as to himself. Harry Mavor drew and painted skilfully. He read to his sons: the Bible, Shakespeare, Browning, Ruskin, Darwin. He took them on expeditions and to the theatre. In his later years — he died at the age of fifty-six of pernicious anaemia — he worked day and night to define a dynamic theory of the ship's propeller, teaching himself the necessary mathematics as he went on. He had earlier invented an electrical reversing gear for diesel ships and invested most of his available cash in building and equipping a cargo ship to demonstrate it. The gear worked perfectly but the ship, on its first voyage to Spain, broke down. Its perishable cargo was lost and the Harry Mavors virtually bankrupted. (The frequency of a severe parental financial crisis in the childhood of future playwrights — for example, Shakespeare, Ibsen, Chekhov, Pirandello — would make a good thesis subject.) They survived, and the First World War, which was soon to break out, was to offer plenty of work for engineers. The two younger sons — Eric, the youngest, after returning wounded from the War — went into the business. Mrs Mavor lived until 1926.

One Way of Living is a strange autobiography. Osborne Mavor describes at considerable length both his school and university days, virtually omits the First World War, and brings the book to a conclusion with a brief and sketchy account of some of his early experiences as a playwright. Clearly, even at the age of five, he had developed an observant eye and that passionate interest in the oddities of behaviour of his contemporaries which fuelled the bubbling creativity which was to produce some forty plays in twenty years. His early years being so fully recorded there, however, it seems unnecessary to deal at length with them again. As I attended both the institutions of his formal education, however, I may perhaps offer a few comments.

The Glasgow Academy (erstwhile described as 'for the Sons of Gentlemen') stands four square in the centre of a dusty desert of gravelly grounds above the river Kelvin in the West End of Glasgow. Internally, iron-palinged balconies surround — or surrounded — a large kind of forum where mornings began with prayers for the whole school, conducted by the Headmaster, and concluding with the Lord's Prayer. When I went, in 1930, to the school this was the most alarming experience of my young life. The words seemed caught up and made indistinguishable in a rushing wind, a susurrus that seemed to come from everywhere and from nowhere. Was it heralding Elijah's chariot?

It was the presence of a distinctly Old Testament God, personified in the portraits of previous Headmasters and sanctified by my father's repeated stories, which made the Glasgow Academy, for me, the locus of a terror deeper and more threatening even than the crowds of horrid, noisy small boys who inhabited it. My brother and I walked to school a mile or so from Woodlands Terrace on the other side of the West End (now Kelvingrove) Park. We debouched from a covered passageway through the old Kelvinside Station into a Hell of shouting gangs of the confident sons of the Glasgow bourgeoisie.

If small Glasgow Academy boys tended to be a little wild and violent, I was among the least violent and the least wild. Few events later in life have inspired in me a greater feeling of dread, of despair at the ignorant bestiality of men, the coarse insensitivity of the human race, than the unmotivated snatching of school caps — naturally in those days one wore a uniform, to lose any item of which meant disgrace — and the careless throwing of them into the street or over the nearest wall. The streets leading off the Great Western Road towards the Academy were, at the hours of arrival and departure, peopled with weeping, capless, small boys, Rachels weeping for their children and unable to be comforted.

I hated the school which my father had, in his way, been able to enjoy. It, like everything else, was probably better before the War. And such schools were perhaps of all institutions the most hard hit

Cartoon of Hamlet as journalist, by Mavor.

by the 1914-18 War. On Remembrance Day the school gathered in the forum. The smaller children were ushered into a strange classroom off the balcony. The door was left open and the elderly master sat gloomily, even tearfully, at his desk; and great waves of song rose from below and thundered through the packed classrooms:

> Time, like an ever-rolling stream,
> Bears all its sons away.
> They fly, forgotten, as a dream
> Dies at the opening day.

In 1914 you left school. You joined the Highland Light Infantry.

You got a pip on your shoulder. You wore the kilt. You got shot down at Ypres or on the Somme. That dark brown panelled hall in the middle of school, those playgrounds, the awful lavatories, what you had learned from these same schoolmasters, that was it for most of you. That was your life.

And in return the masters kept, even in that morgue of a building, something of you. A sense of high hearts, of grand emprise. The names on the still new War Memorial must have been as alive to most of the masters as the shining, impertinent faces answering morning roll-call. They had taught their predecessors Greek verbs and algebra and the Kings of England. There didn't seem much else to do, now, but go on.

After a couple of years, my brother and I were transferred to a Preparatory School on the other side of Glasgow, so I was not there long enough, or was too young, to absorb the school's ethos. But I have the sense that then, and never again, I was in close touch with the real Glasgow bourgeoisie to which the Mavors really belonged. I sensed, no more, its merits, its virtues, felt its hot breath on my face.

3

Glasgow University was founded in 1451. Five hundred years later some friends and I were wandering about near the bottom of the Kelvin Way waiting for the torchlight procession to arrive from the City Chambers. From the end of Sauchiehall Street where I was born there came a band of flickering lights which swelled into a brilliant blaze as several hundred students with torches illuminated the red sandstone walls of the narrow street. At the head, in his gold and black robes, was Walter Elliot, the Rector of the University and, from their university days on, my father's closest friend, although he neglected his own substantial literary gifts to pursue a distinguished career in politics. He said to me, 'This is the best poem I ever composed', and, regarding the University, a rather severe Gothic Revival spire and cluster of vaguely clerical buildings standing on its hill overlooking the West End Park, with five searchlights casting vertical beams behind it to mark the Quincentenary, one couldn't but agree. It *was* rather magnificent.

At the age of eight, in 1933, I had watched, from the summit of the Park, across the valley of the Kelvin, a Rectorial fight and, I think for the first time, had been conscious of a link between my own, totally confusing, life and that of my father and his enormous and important friends who had been in the First World War and who seemed to be busy running the world. From a mile's distance I saw the clouds of flour and soot, the massing of troops, the forbidding black, gargoyle-encrusted walls of the University as marking a place to which I should go. When I did, I found that the Mavor-Elliot period was, still, regarded as a Golden Age. We spoke much of the Corporate Life. We resented the trend which was reducing the University to a training school. We hated the little

A Heated Altercation between Dr Teacher and Dr Findlay on a recent Article in The Tailor and Cutter.

girls who just wanted to qualify and become teachers. We longed for the *ante-bellum* time when students cared more for coffee and conversation and less for classes and degrees, and we attempted, with little success, to revive it, in the middle of another war, through the pages of the *Glasgow University Magazine*.

And, indeed, that period was a distinguished one in the annals of the University. As it is time we brought our protagonist to centre stage, let him describe his own position at that time. It comes from *One Way of Living*:

Round about my twentieth birthday I woke up and became something different. I was a tallish, skinny youth, and if it had

Sir William Macewen remembering Dr Mackintosh's
name but failing completely to recollect his face.

Caricatures by Mavor of members of the Medical Faculty at Glasgow, from a portfolio of cartoons published by him in 1914. National Library of Scotland.

not been for my bulbous head I could have passed through an alderman's thumb-ring. As my allowance of sixty pounds a year was supposed to cover books, clothing and other necessities, and as I was mildly extravagant, I developed a slight eccentricity in dress, thus making a vice of necessity. I wore a battered bowler hat with a hole in the crown. I wore a red necktie, a jacket the colour of tomato soup, a waistcoat from another suit and a pair of magenta trousers striped with mauve which had belonged to my grandfather. My socks were blue with horizontal black stripes, and my shoes were brown brogues. As if this were not enough I also wore a monocle. I am happy to say that this *ensemble* was effective and I became very highly respected about the University growing, at one time, to the dimensions of a myth. Instead of listening to conversation, I began to monopolise it. Additions to the University Union

Drawing by Mavor for *Glasgow University Magazine*, depicting the editorial committee. By permission of Glasgow University Library.

included a quiet little room for the secretary in a far corner of the building. In this room I sat with my feet on the mantelpiece day in and day out and arbitrated on the elegances while a succession of secretaries tore their hair over their accounts. With a number of colleagues I invented several traditional habits for Glasgow University students. Many of these still persist and are solemnly traced back to the fifteenth century by the more historically minded of the undergraduates.

Osborne Mavor's formal field of study was Medicine. His real field, however, was the eccentricities of his colleagues and teachers. Whatever the charms of the Secretary's Room, the wild excitements of Rectorial Elections, of the Officers' Training Corps, walks, talks and camping expeditions, the centre of his interests became the *Glasgow University Magazine* to which he contributed drawings, light verse and funny stories. He became its editor and around it there gathered a remarkable company of kindred spirits.

I think they represented a peculiarly Glaswegian revision of the Aesthetic Movement. Flowing collars and lilies were replaced by damp raincoats and flat caps. The lounges of seedy hotels and waiters with hernias stood in for Elysian fields and Ganymedes. If the G.U.M. crowd didn't always burn with a hard, gem-like flame on a corner of Argyle Street, the spirit was the same. Over a bottle of wine in Walter Elliot's flat, art was valued for art's sake. Politics were not taken seriously. It is reported that when, later, Elliot received a telegram in the trenches asking if he would stand for parliament he replied, 'Yes. Which side?'

A major extension of the artistic interests of the twenty-year-old Mavor and his friends was the Glasgow Repertory Theatre, founded in the early wake of Miss Horniman's achievements with the Abbey Theatre, Dublin, and the Manchester Rep. Alfred Wareing launched the Glasgow Repertory Theatre in April 1909 with Shaw's *You Never Can Tell*, and continued to present Chekhov, Ibsen and Shaw to a not-very-appreciative Glasgow public until the 1914-18 War. But of Wareing there will be more later. He was a companionable man and a passionate propagandist for the theatre.

As an evocation of the spirit of the times, and of that brief golden age at Glasgow University, also as a link with the more serious matters which loomed like a dark thundercloud over its later years, let me end with a description, from *One Way of Living*, of the genesis

Sketches by Mavor of the Glasgow University Officers' Training Corps,
1912-13. By permission of Glasgow University.

ILKLEY · 1913 ·

GAILES
SHORNCLIFFE
STOBS
BARRY
CHATHAM
STIRLING

THE CHAPLAIN

THE
MAJOR

THE
BRIGADIER

RUSTIC REVELRY

of 'Ygorra', the song which is to Glasgow University what 'La Marseillaise' is to the French.

At Lochranza in Arran there were gathered together Alfred Wareing, George Fletcher, Arthur Wallace, Walter Elliot and myself. We were living in a tent by the side of a burn. We followed George Fletcher's definition of camping, which is that one surrounds oneself with every conceivable discomfort and then drinks bottled beer to forget them. Apart from one bright day when I swam out to a yacht in the fairway and was nearly drowned by the undertow on the way back, it rained steadily all week. Among other things Arthur Wallace told us of a colleague of his on the *Manchester Guardian* who had just come back from a Welsh Eisteddfod. He had heard sung there an extraordinary song which, so far as Arthur could remember, went as follows:

> Salasava, salasava,
> Cora Bella, Cora Bella,
> Ching, ching, ching, O.
> Lloyd George Ygorra
> Lloyd George Ygorra
> Ygorra, Ygorra, Ygorra
> YGORRA.

Neither he nor his friend knew what it was about, but there was a vague idea that Ygorra meant, 'He is a great man'.

Now it happened that, through a set of circumstances I shall explain later, Mr Lloyd George was a candidate for the Lord Rectorship of Glasgow and I was one of his supporters. His opponents were Lord Curzon and Mr Keir Hardie. Elliot, I think, fought for Curzon and voted for Keir Hardie, but he had no objection to assisting in the candidature of Mr Lloyd George. He and I foisted the song on the Liberal Club, explaining that it was Welsh for:

> Hail to the Saviour of his People!
> He is a man of war and at the same time of peace.
> He is the Protector of the Poor.
> Lloyd George is a very great man, indeed.

The song was duly sung throughout the election. Lloyd George was defeated but the song did not die. About this time the Officers' Training Corps was instituted by Mr Haldane, and 'Ygorra' came in handy as a marching song. The next Rectorial Election it was sung by both parties indifferently. In 1914 the war broke out and nearly every Highland student in Glasgow enlisted in Lochiel's Camerons. One day, in the winter of 1914, I was standing on Laffan's Plain, near Aldershot, with the Ninth and Fourteenth Divisions of Kitchener's Army. I was with the Fourteenth. The melting snow was over my boot tops and I, with twenty thousand other men, was soaked to the skin. The sleet was falling steadily. We had been there for three hours, waiting for Lord Kitchener and M. Millerand. What with the sleet and the steamy fog it was impossible to see anybody but the battalion in front. But we kept, in our misery, a vague impression that the plain was full of soldiers. The seeping sleet fell, silently blanketing all sounds but occasional grunts of distress and invocations to the Redeemer from the suffering troops. Suddenly, from miles away, on the right, I heard 'Ygorra'. The Camerons were singing it to keep themselves warm.

By the time of the battle of Loos our Highland recruits from Glasgow had all been killed or translated to commissions: but Lochiel's Camerons went over the top dribbling footballs and singing a song that puzzled their officers very much. I am told a piper played the accompaniment. Their Chaplain wrote to the papers about it after the War, and the song he had managed, by listening carefully, to transcribe in some sort of mangled version, was Arthur Wallace's 'Ygorra'.

4

As I have said, my father's autobiography avoids the First World War. He offers instead a supposed conversation between Athos, Porthos and Aramis twenty years after. Their after-dinner conversation is about excellent dinners they enjoyed. Athos describes a recipe for a Tangerine Sling he invented, concocted from claret and rum. When Aramis ventures an anecdote about the War, Athos proposes that they join the ladies.

But the War was, of course, a major influence on the recently qualified doctor, and on the future dramatist. After a period as Resident to Dr Jack at the Royal Infirmary, Dr Mavor picked up his papers for the Special Reserve on the 3rd August 1914. The next day war was declared and two months later he found himself at Tweseldown Camp, near Aldershot, training Royal Army Medical Corps personnel and waiting to get to France.

During the War, Lieutenant Mavor wrote, often several times a week, to his mother. His letters are careful and anxious to cause minimal alarm — he was always aware of his audience. I shall do little more than present, with occasional editorial comments, a brief selection. They tell their own story, one which was almost totally omitted from *One Way of Living*. As prelude I offer one letter each from his father and his mother, both written during that boring spell before he crossed the Channel and joined the War.

His father wrote on 11th October, 1914.

> My Dear Son,
> We are just as wae to miss you as you are to be removed from us. Why fret yourself about the methods of the St John's Ambulance Association? Had you not better give your pupils

Mavor in 1913.

something in which you have confidence? There seems to be plenty of material for your fellowship to work upon and it seems a pity that you should feel that you are wasting your time. Why do you not assume the responsibility of doing your bit as God gives you the light upon it? Do not forget that you have had no field experience and that the S.J.A. people have. The table-napkin drill may not be so silly as it seems to you.

I am again on my back unable to walk many steps but Mackenzie [Ivy Mackenzie, his physician and a lifelong

Lieut. O. H. Mavor, R.A.M.C., at Glasgow, 1914.

friend of Osborne's] satisfies me that this is not surprising or disquieting and we are fairly cheerful.

I have been taking Mackenzie for drives and prescribing a little stimulant in his diet, introducing him to the gustatory joys of the Oyster Bar and trying to broaden him out a bit. Come back soon to comfort your mother and me.

H.A.M.

On the same date his mother writes:

Son o' Mine,

I meant this to be a long letter but alas alas 'the best laid schemes etc.' What sent mine agley was a long sleep in the afternoon, and then I was dancing attendance on Dad who complains he sees so little of me when I am busy. He is well now but still weak on his legs and not able for business this week yet. Eric has got his kilt and looks a great swell. . . .

Oh, how I wish it was all over and I had you all home again. I want you boys and I want you so much esp. on Sunday nights. Aunt Mary and Eric and I sang No 339 and then I read 17 Exodus and 6 Ephesians from 10th verse then 103 Psalm. I wonder if Jack and you are remembering to read with us on Sundays. I sent you the Weekly Herald and will do so regularly if you care to have it. Let me know. I have not been able to get communication with Stobhill started yet, but am remembering. They are so busy they have overflowed into the Royal Infirmary. Dr Andrews was telling Uncle John that many have made wonderful escapes and that on the whole the wounds are not so serious as might be expected.

My love to you my lad — remember Whose you are and Whom you serve, and that the man of prayer is not easily beaten by anything. Pray for yourself and brothers and think of the prayers and love of your

Mother

Although the 42nd Field Ambulance was brought up to strength and ready to go in October, nothing much happened until six or seven months later. On 21st May 1915, my father had written:

I'm sorry to hear that Dad has not been so well again, but, as the Doctor says, it's a common enough thing to happen in that kind of trouble and is not a thing to be too anxious about though it looks a little alarming at first. Tell him he'll win through all right, and that he's three times the reserve of strength now that he had a month or two ago.

I saw James Barr's death in *The Times* this morning. It's very sad, but weighed against a University career it turns the scale easily. I thought about Teddy Maitland that it was a fortunate kind of death too. 'To carry back bright to the coiner the mintage of Man', and to have a young, strong, untroubled angel in the Heaven of people's memories. I should think his father and mother would be more proud than sad.

Down here we are still marking time in hopes of an early move but there is nothing beyond a myriad rumours to hint about where we're going. . . .

I'll let you know all right when I go and send my address. About the place — if I put two points of exclamation (!!) the first letters of the sentence after that will spell the name. e.g. What about this!! You'll please remember Eric's socks. [Ypres. The cipher will be useful to the biographer.]

With my dear love to you and Dad.

In *One Way of Living* my father relates 'At last a staff officer on a motor cycle arrived through the pouring rain a little after midnight. There was a light in my hut and he hammered at my door. Twenty-four hours later we were curled round the legs of a saloon table on the way to Havre, soaked to the skin and trying to get to sleep. Four hours after that I saw through the porthole the scarlet trousers of a French sentry'.

On 21st May, he wrote to his mother:

I am now at or within a dozen miles of this Front we all hear so much about, and beyond a sound as of distant coalheavers loading up a cellar, there is little to indicate that this is so. The sun is shining just the same and the village is like any other dirty village. . . .

We had a long train journey after we debarked and saw that France is a bonny, bonny spot. Part we went through had a ladylike prettiness I've never seen anywhere else. And the magpie was the prevailing bird, and the prevailing men were in blue coats and red breeks, and the prevailing children were very agile and graceful and friendly and impudent — I don't know why Germans kill them.

We have now entered the bully beef zone!! Now, when our fine young persons regard eating stew as the usual state of things it comes hard on them to eat tunny sandwiches. [Cipher: N.W. of Ypres.]

I may write more interesting letters when I see more of the War, but I don't think so. I'll likely be a very tired youth in the times off. But I'll let you know how I'm getting on as regularly as I can and I'll certainly write a longer letter next time. . . .

Ten days later he was posted to take charge of an Officers' Rest Station in the chateau Mont Noir, 'on the [French-Belgian] frontier . . . and from the top of the hill we can see Ypres burning and Armentiers burning and St Eloi burning and a lot of other little towns burning, and away in the south Neuve Chapelle. The guns shake the windows at night . . .' The next stop was Vlamertinghe, almost a suburb of Ypres, west of the town.

I was sleeping in the school house at Vlamertinghe. I had ridden in to it on a large horse called Ikey, from a fancied resemblance to a great financier. It had been a bright, sunny day and all that could be seen of a war was an aeroplane flying high and surrounded by dabs of cotton wool. The houses were a little battered and the *pavé* was disturbed in places. We cleaned out the school house and established a dressing station and went to sleep. I was awakened by an unpleasant tearing sound. It was partly screech and partly whistle, and the main impression it made on my half-awakened mind was that whatever caused the sound was angry at me and wanted to get me. It was followed by a loud bang that shook the floor and rattled the little windows. These sounds and their climaxes followed each other with great rapidity and I sat up in my sleeping bag in some consternation. The door opened and Sergeant Gatehouse, a schoolmaster in civil life, put his intelligent face round the door. He said in the army voice he had been at some pains to cultivate during the eight months' training at Tweseldown,

'I have to report, sir, that this dressing station is being consistently shelled.'

'In that case,' I said, 'I'd better get up.'

I found my little advance party in greatcoats and balaclava helmets standing in the roadway in the misty May dawn. They were looking at the church a few hundred yards down the road. Against the church steeple and in the graveyard round it, light shells were bursting in salvos of four. We stood and coughed and smoked cigarettes and inhaled the throat-catching rime for about twenty minutes, and then they stopped. . .

As I stood there chewing my cigarette on that May dawn

Sketch by Mavor of a dressing station, 1915.

I thought to myself, 'I don't know. I'm not sure. But it looks to me as if this business might quite easily become intolerable.' It did. . . .

(One Way of Living)

As Lieutenant, later Captain, Mavor was to spend the rest of 1915 in and around Ypres it is worth recording the general state of that part of the Front, which ran almost due south from the Channel through Ypres, took a quick curve round Armentiers and then stretched south-west through Loos and south through Arras to the Somme.

In April the battle line had been drawn north and south through Ypres, more or less along the natural line of the Yser-Lys canal. There was, however, a substantial bulge in the line, protecting Ypres, the British lines at that point having established themselves seven or eight miles to the east of the town. The north part of the bulge was held by two French divisions, who were therefore on the British left.

On 22nd April at five o'clock in the evening there began a furious German bombardment of the town and, simultaneously, a great greenish-yellow cloud drifted over the French lines. This was chlorine gas and, in no time, there was a four-mile gap in the lines inhabited only by the dead and the dying. Coughing and suffocating, the rest of the defence had fled back to the canal. The astonishing effectiveness of this new weapon surprised the German commanders, who were not ready to press home their advantage; but Ypres was now an easy target and was soon shelled to pieces. The salient to the east of the town was to remain a much-contested battlefield for nearly three more years. It was exposed and difficult to defend and it may be that it would have been wiser to withdraw to the natural defensive line of the canal. The names given to parts of the salient — most of them within a mile or two of the town — tell their own story: Hellblast Corner, Shrapnel Corner, Sanctuary Wood.

16th June, 1915

I seem to be fated never to write those nice picturesque 'eyewitness' letters I meant to once. I can't tonight because I'm too sleepy as I was up all night yesterday dressing hundreds of wounded from the Somethingth Battle of Ypres.

I'm O.C. a Dressing Station in a sort of Church School not very far back because our guns shoot over our heads, and we had a Rush last night. Most were fairly bad wounds but the men were very cheery and enthusiastic and said they had beaten the Germans and killed enormous numbers and the Germans were afraid of them, and our gunners were rotten, and they, the infantry, were very fine chaps. As indeed they were. . . . It was a good tonic for people not very pleased with human nature, to see our orderlies dog-tired with physical and mental labour absolutely mothering these chaps who had called them the Rob All My Comrades at Aldershot. . . .

21st June, 1915

I went up the night before last to a certain big ruined city [Ypres] on the German edge of which we have an Advanced Dressing Station. It is about the size of Paisley. I never had a more extraordinary drive.

It was a fine moonlight night and still, very still, and

Sketch by Mavor on the Western Front.

after we passed the town-gate it was like moving in a dream through the City of the Dead. Half the buildings are down in heaps of fine dust and the others stand like beautiful grey skeletons.

At the other end we tumbled out of our cars into a cellar where we sat most of the night and heard the shrapnel whacking on the *pavé*.

I had to clear out with the cars before dawn and just when the sky began to brighten in the middle of a British bombardment the tyre of my car burst and we had to sit in a ditch and watch the motormen work as they hadn't worked before. And so home.

26th June, 1915

I'm writing this under a pear tree in the most excellent sunshine and peace of mind. The blue carnations grow in the wheat and the pungent smell of guano wafts through the air, rendering it a trifle balmy. The fields here are intensively cultivated right up to the roadside ditches and that's all my war news.

We are back some miles from the bang shop taking a pretty well-earned rest. These rests are the only discoverable advantage of trench warfare. . . . And you shouldn't read what blethering parsons write to the News. I've got loads of far better stories than that cutting. And I've no admiration for that 'Surgeon-Major' (whatever rank that is) who took 20 hours to get through 200 cases. I'll whisper and risk the censor what we got through our Dressing Station between 3 p.m. and 4.30 a.m. on our big day last week. Only don't let it go abroad. Thirteen hundred and fifteen. We got two officers up from the 44th to help us, some of ours being in other jobs, and they went back and said I was the only one who did any work. While this agrees with my private opinion, it is not quite accurate.

Anyway, we're all glad to get back here, because anyone who says he is really fond of working all night is as big a liar as anyone who says he likes shell-fire, and that's saying a lot. . . .

30th June, 1915

We are still in the orchard and nothing quaint, soul-stirring or alarming has broken the perfection of our perfect peace. Satan is finding mischief with wild and usually optimistic rumours — the one which we find too blissful to be true being that we're going south for our next endeavour. Our brigade doesn't like its small corner in the very least. But the Germans like it very much less. Both armies beg to be allowed to fight anywhere else. Even for us, who are pretty far back, it is an alarming sort of place, though not unbearably so. Back in the orchard, however, we're not alarmed by anything except that the greengages and cherries will soon be ripe and then we'll have to resist temptation.

19th July, 1915

I just got the telegram about poor old Dad today at midday. It came as a shock though it wasn't quite unexpected. It was a kindly death after all to come when there was so little left in life. Winter would have been terrible and we ought to be glad that he went out in the sunshine among the flowers.

20th June, 1915

I got your letter today. I'm glad that Dad went out so

31

peacefully and happily. I should think he knew. He was never afraid of anything and there was no reason why he should fear death.

He kept his boys turned towards things pure, lovely and of good report and we'll always be grateful and keep his memory green. And so will a very great number of other people he was an inspiration and guide to.

We're back at work, now, I'm glad to say.

2nd August, 1915

We're quieting down here a bit after the 115th Battle of Y——. Some say that they ran and some say that we ran and some say that nane ran at a', man. It doesn't look a very big battle in the papers but it was here, and the Germans don't seem to have made much of a pretty fierce attack. I'm very glad to have been in it if only for one night — almost as glad as I was to get out of it or ever the pale moon set.

It was guns and guns and guns and bewilderment as to our whereabouts and more guns and twa' three bullets running through the wood and through the wood but not killing very many muckle men just while we were there, for a knock on the funny-bone for one of our bearers was all our trouble. And the moon shone very bright and the shells roared and crashed and nobody was frightened — only a little anxious. This isn't a very clear picture but only very good or very bad writers should be allowed to tell about the war.

In *One Way of Living* he writes: 'I wish you had seen all the guns of Ypres opening fire on the morning when the Bosche first put over blazing treacle when I was wandering about Sanctuary Wood'. This was about a mile on the wrong side of Ypres, to the south-east. Captain Mavor was to be there again for a week or two, right in the front line, in a regimental aid post, and in another battle.

September 1915 began with a new air of excitement that spread the whole length of the Allied Front. A great attack was to be launched which would set the Allies on the road to Berlin. The British end of the attack was the Battle of Loos. It was finally launched on 23rd September and it was a disaster. The gas blew in the wrong direction and mud, muddle, and almost total confusion about what was expected of the front-line troops, combined with the German superiority of small-arms fire, led to a much-worsened situation which was only retrieved by the advent of winter weather. The 42nd Field Ambulance did not, as far as I can discover, move south to Loos. But there was a simultaneous battle in the salient, with similar results.

26th September, 1915

Well, I think the waur o' it's bye for the time being. At least I hope to God it is, for it's been an ugly time. I mayn't tell you what's happened here just yet except that both sides were beaten in turn and nothing done locally, but it's been a big thing in old Papa's strategy.

However, I'm still alive and cheerful in a rather depopulated salient.

I'll tell you the whole story later on as far as I know it from the Advanced Dressing Station point of view. I'm busy not thinking about it at all just now. . . .

29th September, 1915

I don't want to write about the battle because I want to get the blood and mud and wet out of my head, but you may as well know that on the 23rd I went up and formed an Advanced Dressing Station at the place where I had my aid post when I was with the regiment. And shelling and banging went on all night and all the next day; and on the morning of the 25th, after I had dropped off to sleep in a chair, it began to be properly loud and they went over swish swish all over. And by and by the wounded began to come in. It was the most pitiful, terrible sight in the whole world. The noise went on and our bearers went up and cleared the fire trenches by daylight which isn't usually done. I stayed 1,000 yards or so behind and I'm glad I was put there. Two of our officers have earned D.S.O.s, whether they get them or not, and the 42nd covered itself with glory; the other Ambulances weren't in it. Well, I messed about there being a kind of stage-manager and slinging wounded after wounded along the Menin road on wheeled stretchers and swearing at people for messing round the door and dressing and listening to the shrapnel and writing notes; and thus passed 4 days.

It seems we were working some sort of feint up here to let

Papa get in with his right down south. Anyway the Bosche piled up his best against us and it was nasty while it lasted. We had 1 man killed and about 6 wounded, which is R.A.M.C. luck, for our bearers were strolling rapidly across the open at times when the infantry were crouching in dug-outs. And the Bosche whizz-banged any stretcher-party they saw. He only behaved like a gentleman once. The day before yesterday 2 Saxons got over the parapet to bring in some of the wounded who lay between the trenches. And our men mistook what they were after and fired on them, so they hopped back. And then an officer who spoke German shouted across that he was very sorry and might we bring them in, please? So they allowed 2 of our men to go over by daylight and the wounded were brought in. But the Saxons are very nice lads and very friendly.

This is not a good description of a battle but it is not meant to be. . . .

October brought a brief leave and the winter was spent in a canvas hut in a sea of mud, still within earshot of the guns, looking after cases of scabies, louse-infestations and trench-fever. It had been a hard year since Dr Mavor had travelled so lightheartedly down to Aldershot to join Kitchener's Army.

5

With the Spring, the 42nd Field Ambulance were on the move again. First to the French border town of Wormhout: 'I think we'll be comfortable here but we'll probably have some rows with the chatelaine!! When officers raid men's houses one unfastens the bulldog!' And then to Amiens: 'It's snowing — of all things to happen with the crocuses out!!

> "Not even 'appy roamin;
> And men in exile never smile. . . ." '

(It is entertaining to think of earnest students, unaware of the cipher, trying to find the source of Captain Mavor's quotation.)

The letters describing the following year are not dissimilar to those of 1915. Rather than risk wearying the reader I will offer only two segments of the correspondence.

The first is interesting as an example of the writer or, more particularly, the kind of writer Bridie was to become, and his relationship with the truth, or his manipulation of that tricky concept. The truth was overrich in experience. The reporting of it was, by today's unbuttoned standards, hermetic in the extreme. The audience, however, was his mother. To her he wrote, on 31st May 1916:

> I'm sitting under a cherry-tree in heavenly weather and blooming health. Everything is peaceful except for popping anti-aircraft Archibalds and, every quarter of an hour or so, the mellow note of a Whizz-bang calling to its mate.
>
> The night before last I was very frightened. I was orderly officer and, as the night was quiet, I went to bed about half-past

eleven and was just drowsing gently towards midnight when the unholiest row I had heard since the 25th of September brought me broad awake. The night before we had been 'drilling the Boche' — which means giving him just the sort of blazes he gets before an attack at some ungodly hour of the night. Well, on Tuesday night the spirit of emulation seized him and he let off on *our* trenches. This made all our batteries open fire, and after several wildly disgusted shots at them (our batteries) he called 'Dirty brat' and went to bed for the night. However satisfactory this was from the military point of view, it was a great worry to at least one medical practitioner who lay in bed and thought of the various parts of him he would *not* like the roof to fall on, or nose-caps to come through the window at.

While the passage reeks of *suppressio veri* and *suggestio falsi* it is intended to reassure the writer's mother, but *also* to mark, somehow, in some sort of detoxified way, the fact that he escaped death by a hairsbreadth.

It is only on the fourth page of his next letter, of 9th June, after descriptions of a jolly evening in the Mess, the reddening of the cherries in the back garden, and regrets at the death of Kitchener, that we have:

> About the woollens. You mind I told you about the shelling round our old Mess. Well, a whizz-bang insinuated itself in at my bedroom window and I am afraid what's left of the woollens (which were under the window) is hardly worth sending home. I wasn't in the bedroom at the time or I'd have had an excellent Blighty. I am afraid such luck is not in my way.
>
> My good new breeks were also put on the sick list with my sweater and leather waistcoat. . . .

In *One Way of Living* we get, I assume, the true story:

> King and I . . . were sitting by the fireside in an Arras music master's house. The front windows of our room opened on the pleasant Quai de Caserne, the back on a tangled garden and a glass-roofed porch. We were having our bedtime toddy and the Germans were shelling a 75 Battery along the street. All of a sudden a shell hit our house and down came the glass

porch. King crouched under the windowsill and I sat down in an arched doorway, while the air became full of flashes and bangs and clatterings. We then bethought ourselves of our faithful batmen who slept upstairs and were rushing to their aid when they knocked us backwards downstairs. They were wrapped in blankets. We adjourned to the cellar, but it was full of water, and the shelling soon stopped.

My room on the first floor was full of moonlight and I walked on two inches of finely powdered dust. The blanket window-screen had been blown in and the nose-cap had gone through my bed at the point where my umbilicus would have been if I hadn't persuaded King to have one more toddy. . . .

Summer brought battles on the Somme. The plan was simple. The German trenches were to be pulverised by bombardment and then the troops were to flow across in their thousands, opening a breach in the Line and a clear road to Berlin. Like Loos it was a disaster. The German trenches were not pulverised. The British troops attacked up a hill across a valley of the Somme, highly exposed and subjected to devastating gunfire from the well-established enemy. At enormous cost a few hundred yards were captured over a period of weeks and months. Captain Mavor was posted as a surgical specialist to a Corps Clearing Station eight or nine miles behind the fire trenches:

28th June, 1916

The most interesting item of news refers to a working in the strange mind of our Colonel. As I told you, we've got a surgical outfit (including a specialist). Well, he's made up his mind to make me assistant surgical specialist. The gentleman he's got on the job is rather old and fussy and is there on the strength of having said that he had done major operations. The process of reasoning, I take it, is that I'm comparatively young, the reverse of fussy (as I sit in a chair all day and frequently go to sleep) and have never at any time claimed to know anything whatever about surgery. . . .

11th August, 1916

I am writing this in bed at eleven a.m. I'm not going to get up before 11.30 a.m. as it is not worth while, there being nothing to do and nowhere to go. I lunch at 12.30 and start work at 1 p.m. From there my shift goes on till 9 p.m. I have dinner and at about 11 slide off to bed to sleep the round of the clock. I like this kind of work quite well, as when you get to a certain stage in this war your two great cries are (1) cut and dried work, and (2) plenty of sleep.

We are in tents on a hillside in a fairly ugly bit of country. . . .

15th August, 1916

I'm getting a little bit nippier with my surgery and don't feel such a criminal when I do anything to a patient. Our work here is partly to take the burden off the Casualty Clearing Stations and partly to give all wounds that early and radical treatment they appear to need. We remove all injured tissue and bits of shrapnel and things and make as much as possible big, free-draining, surgical wounds instead of the little closed-up gangrene-patches that most wounds here are. We don't do anything to head or abdominal wounds, wounds of the knee-joint, or compound fractures of the legs. This narrows the work down to tying arteries, amputations and free incision and drainage which, after all, I'm fairly competent to do after my hospital experience.

21st August, 1916

I got your long letter yesterday but had no time to answer it and today I'm awful sleepy. I've been working like blazes — operating 16 hours a day for the past 2 or 3 days and have been sleeping most of my off time. It's my private opinion that we try to do rather too much at this Dressing Station, but it's good experience and does a lot of good to the British soldiers in a very great many cases. My operative dexterity has gone up a very great deal. I'm getting rather a blood at amputations though I don't approve of them except as a counsel of despair. I did two yesterday — one on a Private Geordie Robinson, late of Govan and Fairfield's, and another on a Boche prisoner. I did Geordie's beautifully with no haemorrhage at all. I'm sorry to say that he died and the dirty Boche lived and is going strong.

The work is hard and rather straining on the nerves as the responsibility is pretty heavy, but I'm glad to say (and touching wood) that it's not mixed up with shell-fire. That would make it unbearable. Of course I've done longer spells, and done it under pretty heavy explosive work from the Boche side, but it's been mere dresser's work — not like this. . . .

17th September, 1916

To my no small disgust, believe me, I'm still attached to the Corps and am up to my eyes in the most dismal kind of work. Hours 1 p.m. on the 15th to 6 p.m. on the 16th, at which time I went to bed and slept the sleep of the as-just-as-possible till 3.30 a.m. this morning, since when I have been pushing around. This is, of course, pie to a lot of the work I've had to do now and again since I came out, but I feel like a subtle compound of a wet dishcloth and an influenzal cold. . . .

By the end of the month he was back with the Field Ambulance and his two and a half years on the Western Front petered out with a series of jobs at Advanced Dressing Stations, at Rest Camps, as temporary Second-in-Command, as temporary Town Major, at a gas course; but he had recurrent attacks of fever and finally jaundice, and was evacuated, by way of Manchester, to Edinburgh and home early in 1917. He had hopes of returning to his Field Ambulance with the rank of Lieutenant-Colonel but, instead, he was posted to Mesopotamia and to a series of Arabian Nights' Entertainments. It was to be perhaps the happiest period of his life.

6

The situation in north-west Persia and the Caucasus in 1917 was, to say the least, complicated. The Germans, aided by their allies the Turks, had a grand scheme to build a railway to the east. The Berlin-Abadan railway, opening on the Persian Gulf, was foiled by the capture of Baghdad by Sir Stanley Maude, and a second plan was evolved to take the railway east through the Caucasus to Baku on the Caspian Sea then east to Bokhara and south through Afghanistan. To forward this scheme the Turks advanced to Tiflis (Tblisi) and found little opposition.

'With the object of upsetting these arrangements', General Dunsterville raised 'a collection of adaptable young men', popularly known as the Hush-hush Brigade, and drove, in a score or two of model-T Fords, from Mesopotamia up through the Paitak Pass, across Persia and to the Caspian. They never did get to Tiflis. The south Caspian coast was largely controlled by one Kuchik Khan, a lively brigand, and north of the Caspian were the Russians, recently driven out of Persia and commanded by Bicherakoff. The year 1917 was, of course, an important one for the Russians, in the throes of their Revolution, and Bicherakoff's command was somewhat diluted by bands of Bolsheviks and Anarchists. There were also roaming packs of Armenians, Georgians, Azerbaijanis, Cossacks and other deviant groups, each with its own solution for a complex destiny.

Dr Alec Glen, a lifelong friend and, later, a Visiting Physician at the Victoria Infirmary, for whom I worked as a Registrar, describes his meeting with Captain Mavor in Mesopotamia:

Like Mavor I trained with a Field Ambulance and went to

Gallipoli in the Spring of 1915. After six months there I went on with my Division to Mesopotamia. I was one of 40 who got leave home in the Summer of 1917 after the capture of Baghdad, because my father was seriously ill and not expected to recover. Believe it or not I had to pay my own fare home in a passenger steamer. Owing to circumstances at home I overstayed my leave and had great difficulty in getting permission to return to my unit. Eventually I succeeded and was posted back to the Mesopotamia Force, although not to my unit.

After the usual fortnight's voyage up the river Tigris by steamer, by good luck I met an ambulance wagon from my old unit in Baghdad. The Turks had apparently disappeared. They had got a new officer, Captain Mavor, in my place who was great fun. He had organised a concert party and had written a play which they were rehearsing at present. I said I thought I knew Captain Mavor.

I soon found that Mavor was one of the focal points of the Division, just as he had been as a student. All sorts of people from Infantry Subalterns to Generals kept popping in. Any excuse was good enough to see what Mavor was doing.

Captain Mavor had sailed from Plymouth, relished the hospitality of Durban (though he didn't like Cape Town) with its evening picnics on the beach, was deputed in India to take some soldiers three thousand miles by train to Peshawar on the north-west frontier, then continued to Delhi, and finally to Mesopotamia, 'the birthplace of the world'.

He wrote a book about his succeeding adventures, called *Some Talk of Alexander*, which marked, in 1926, the first appearance of Mr Bridie as author on the title page. It is an over-stylish book, much influenced by Chester-Bellocism, and one wishes he had written again and more overtly about these amazing times. But we must have a few quotations:

> Next morning we followed a trail of lorries over more hot foothills, and bit the dust by maunds, and so we came to Khaniquin. Khaniquin has suffered from three armies, and lies battle weary in the sunshine. It was hot and dusty and golden green, and a sluggish river full of mules and Arabs meandered through it. I lunched with the Indian Army in a

room like an unfinished cathedral; and then we followed a trail of lorries over hot, dusty roads, and the great hills drew nearer. . . .

At last we saw the true wall of Persia and saw it by the falling sun. Never the maddest vorticist dreamt a thing so ugly and bizarre as that wild range of mountains, with their truncated bluffs, squat tumuli, long searing sandstone and basalt gashes, their pinks and slates and greys all washed with the bloody sunset. Here and there a curve of mountain ridge would begin to sweep with some nobility, only to be brought up short by a solid geometrical joke. Qasri-shirind sat, a solemn bundle of flat cubes done in glaring mud-yellow, patterned all wrong and shrieking to a green bice sky. For such a landscape, you must know, the appropriate drink is whisky (Irish) and chlorinated water, and this I had, and crossed a hill into the darkness. . . .

We awoke at the foot of the Paitak Pass and a huge and lusty wind blew through a plain between immense and righteous mountains. . . . At the summit of the Pass the wind blew clear like crystal and gentle as the hand of a maiden, and the sky was very blue. Down we went again through a gorge to a tableland where the fields were green and the great pink mountains shielded and did not menace. There was one village of gardens and many waters and a night's rest. There were strange bridges and torn hamlets where the Brotherhood of Man had left its footprints as it fled from the Turk — hunger, rape, murder, destruction, disease, and dirt, and then, because we had been good, God showed us Kermanshah in the evening.

O jewelled Persia, dreams of shimmering silks and dropping waters and musk and topazes and zephyrs and honey and myrrh are netted in the soft sound of your name! For one evening those dreams came true.

Behind the little coral town sat a nobly perfect mountain like an Emperor, all mauve and old rose and deep purple shadows draped over beaten gold. Round its noble broad base the gossamer mirage floated, indeed that mysterious river that flows round fair Elfland, seen by John Keats and forded by Thomas of Ercildoune in the twilight. Away to the south — but if I have been fool enough to describe the magic mountain, believe me there are degrees in folly, and no fine writing here will slander these infinite leagues of wonder.

Kermanshah is situated on a mound and surrounded by little towers, in each of which brass-mounted hoboes smoking long wooden pipes pretend to keep the peace. There are groves of poplars before which pose and gesture the inhabitants in perfect harmony with the laws of colour and form. The rich and the bucks and wits promenade in the evening in very small round hats and frock-coats with Presbyterian skirts, and turn grave, innocent, olive countenances to the setting sun. Some wealthy Arabs walk among them in black and green and exquisitely laundered linen, wagging their scarlet beards; and little boys in pyjamas and the tremendous Persian hat, looking like little kings on a chess-board; and sturdy ruffians in faded blue and yellow; and little girls in pink bridal dresses and pearls; and veiled ladies in black and flowered silk; and very poor and starving persons.

We skirted the city's suburbs and avoided its characteristic stinks. Then we came to a gentlemanly broad road and a bridge with pointed arches, below which ran a rushy peacock-blue river. And such was the glamour of that place that the soldiers, as they lit their bivouac fires on the dim and dusty banks, looked not only grand but beautiful.

From this beginning, Persia offered, and Bridie recounts, entertainments out of the *Arabian Nights*. Most of the stories are of simple, decent British soldiery sorting out rich, grand and heavily armed denizens. At one point Captain Mavor was offered, in exchange for an ambulance, first a pearl necklace and then 'the quite magnificent offer of five thousand riflemen with rifles in their hands. If I had believed him, I should have closed with this offer. There was much one could have done at that time in the way of travel, sport and adventure with five thousand riflemen — even Persians. But I thought him an old liar, told him so, and that I held His Majesty's Commission and was not to be bribed.' It turned out that the old liar could well have delivered on his bargain.

Through Persia the unit went to Baku. Dr Glen records that:

It was certainly an amazing city at that time. It had

Sketch by Mavor of *Tosca* at the Baku Opera, 1919.

been raided successively by Russians, Bolsheviks, Armenians, Turks, Tartars and finally the British. Mavor started learning the language as soon as we arrived in Baku. When we were busy during the day he practised on the telephone operators or anyone else who was available. He organised a general hospital for the British troops in a large college. I had charge of a Typhus Hospital in a school. As soon as evening came, Mavor headed for the city. As many of the rest of us who could manage went along also. In a surprisingly short space of time he appeared to be on intimate terms with a very large number of the varied population. For some reason or other they called him 'Dr Jim'. Mavor went everywhere unarmed in that dangerous city without the least feeling of apprehension.

Sketch by Mavor of *La Traviata* at the Baku Opera, 1919.

He was no doubt quite right. Nobody would have done him any harm. He understood them and they all loved him. It was a dangerous city nevertheless. Rifle shots seemed to keep popping off all the time but no one seemed to be much the worse. Bolshevik risings took place and the city lights would go out occasionally due to sabotage in the generating station.

There was a very fine opera house with a permanent company who played a different opera nearly every night. The routine was to go to the opera and afterwards go to the Casino (a restaurant with a cabaret show) for supper. Mavor loved the Casino. He met the 'villagers' there. When the Tartars and Russians approved the show they fired their revolvers through

45

Sketches by Mavor at Baku 1919.

the roof to show their appreciation.

Two character-sketches from Bridie's *Some Talk of Alexander*, about the Baku Opera:

Gucassoff, the tenor, was an Armenian. He was tall and slim with a hooked nose, and eyebrows that went up diagonally over his bald brow and almost met in the middle. He sang like a sucking dove in his love scenes and like a fierce tom-cat in his others. We called him Nyet, because the Russian version of 'Faust' begins with that word, and he uttered it with the most stentorian mew you can possibly imagine. He walked always on tiptoe with his arms outspread, palms downward, and elbows crooked, and he wore on most occasions the sweetest expression of countenance; but, when he was counterfeiting rage, he was at once pitiful and terrible. I remember well the

night when a middle-aged mezzo-soprano had journeyed from Tiflis to play Carmen to Nyet's Don Jose. Madame was rather stout, and Madame, except on her beautiful high notes, was rather short of breath. Nyet's customary Carmen was his wife, an excellent comedienne and dancer, and the best Carmen I have ever seen, for all that she sang no better than an old kettle. She was lissom, strong, young and active, and was well used to Nyet's manner of playing the part. With Madame it was different.

Now, Nyet was determined on that night to play, sing, and if necessary, maul the Tiflis prima donna off the stage. I saw real terror in her eyes when, in the last act, Nyet withdrew himself to the extreme corner (O.P.) and stood crouching on tiptoe, with his elbows on a level with his shoulders, his eyes blazing, dribbling tears, the foam gathering at the down-drawn corners of his mouth. Then suddenly with a baresark howl he hurled himself, in two steps and a leap, on poor old Carmen. He threw her a couple of yards by the force of his impact, jumped upon her with both feet, dragged her back to her old stance, pummelled, savaged, bruised, and finally stabbed her. I almost think he bit her too. She took her call looking like the dead indeed. On the next night, the carpenter erected a stout, serviceable tree right in the middle of the Plaza, and to this the diva clung like the lady in the beautiful picture called Rock of Ages, and the mark of Nyet's grip still showed on her buxom shoulders.

The opera was usually late in beginning, like everything else in that singular town. I think they waited for Mischa. Mischa was Bicherakoff's Cornet, a picturesque young man of nineteen, usually *nimnoshka piane* [pleasantly intoxicated], and the life and soul of wherever he went. And he was to be seen everywhere. We saw him at the Kazino weeping into a large table cloth in response to the moans of Horrible Hannah, the tragedienne, from the stage; dancing perilously on the ledge of a box twenty-five feet from the ground; conducting the orchestra at a *conversazione*; casting joyous eyes on the ecstatic flappers of the Boulevard; turning to mirth all things of earth as only boyhood could.

When all the opera-goers were seated, Mischa came down the central aisle. He was spiritually drunk. He floated along the coco-nut matting, swaying and balancing on the toes of his flat-soled Wellingtons, waving gracefully to the ladies, saluting politely to the men. He timed his arrival to the moment when the conductor rapped with his baton as a signal for the overture to start. For three minutes or more the whole theatre waited breathless while Mischa asked for the conductor's wife, his little children, and the state of his liver. Then Mischa kissed the conductor, indicated to the orchestra that they might now proceed, bowed to the audience, saluted a friend whom he had not hitherto noticed, and took his seat in the front row of the stalls, breathing brandy and benignity.

Mischa's patronage of the opera showed evidence of his unerring good taste. The opera was the nicest thing in a not very nice city. If in any way this chapter conveys the impression of a sneer at the courageous artistes who lifted up our hearts for us in the midst of a strange and sordid country, I am sorry. Night after night Russians, Tartars, and Armenians forgot their hunger, poverty, and terror, and we our exile, while these men and women put their whole souls into making beautiful sounds for us. They were no mean artists and they were great people. I wish them well wherever they are.

My father, when I knew him, continued to sing the prelude to Pagliacci and bits of Mephistopheles from *Faust*. We had a few dinner parties where Alec Glen and Bryce McCall Smith used to get a little *nimnoshka piane*, put plates on their heads and sing 'The Droug From Astrakhan'. But Eric Linklater wrote a good description of the Baku Club, a movable feast wherein my father mildly perpetuated his happiest years:

One of Mr Bridie's private jokes was the Baku Club, which he founded. Its membership was never large, and its life was hazardous. The original members were a few officers who had served under Dunsterville on the Caspian shore, and its only function was an annual dinner which every year was held in a different town. The purpose of this itinerancy was to give members the convenience of dining, in the old-fashioned exuberance of Russia, at some distance from their homes; but a further advantage was discovered in the principle when it began to appear that an hotel which had once accommodated a meeting of the club might be reluctant to do so again. Having become a member on the small qualification of a brief and almost accidental sojourn in Baku, I attended a dinner in a quiet and dignified country town. [I think it was in the Cross Keys Hotel in Peebles.] Three or four decent Scotch waiters had been persuaded to wear Cossack dress, and there was plenty of caviare and Riga vodka. There was, perhaps, too much vodka, for during the evening I discovered that a young and frivolous waiter was conducting horrified, mystified, or giggling diners — non-members, that is — to a raree-show in one of the bedrooms, where two portly gentlemen in dignified evening dress, nicely garnished with rows of miniature medals, lay sound asleep upon a double bed. Mr Bridie in a nearby room, was playing accompaniments on the piano for members who wanted to sing; and persuading others, who had not yet reached the stage, that their turn was next. He

'Persian Boy', one of the finest of Mavor's drawings in 1917-18. By permission of the National Galleries of Scotland.

was, I thought, both eager to promote a general merriment, and interested to observe — but with a most kindly curiosity — the manner in which each contributed to it. He would, as it were, first load the gun, then stand a little way apart to observe the shot. Benignity moved him, but criticism was wide awake.

I confess that this quality in my father infuriated me in my youth. I am alarmed to find that friends of my son find me equally infuriating. I think that I am simply trying to draw them out, occasionally disputing their less well-founded assertions; and they assume that they are being mocked. Linklater continues with a personal description too good to exclude:

> He is indeed benign, and obviously so. A recession of his hair has enlarged the expanse of his forehead and exposed the long capacity of his skull: its conformation is undoubtedly benign. But I grow a little diffident when I speak of his personal appearance, for though there are few people in the world of whom I am more fond, I cannot pretend that he is strictly handsome. Impressive, yes. His height is sufficient, his figure has acquired enough weight to give it consequence, and very notable is his frequent expression of preoccupation with some noble, melancholy theme. Far away, one thinks, in the depths of that great head, huge thoughts engage in portentous argument — though in fact they may be whittling into shape some new elaborate joke. His mouth betrays him. His forehead and his dreaming eyes may be impressive, but the corners of his mouth turn sharply upward like quotation marks about a broad incipient grin. His eyes, small behind spectacles, are very lively when they wake from dreaming, and his nose is quite unlike the noses of ordinary men. . . .

It was well into 1919 before Dr Mavor returned from the war and set up in general practice in the Langside district of Glasgow. He was then thirty-one. In *Some Talk of Alexander* he wrote, in a kind of Happy Warrior doggerel, a few lines that I find very moving:

> Then stood I proudly on Galata Bridge
> And said to Orobas: 'This fytte is told.
> It may be we shall founder on the voyage
> That leads us westward to the Happy Isles.

But we have heard the blinded Cyclops roar
And messed among the Anthropophagi.
And ever where we went, our seigneur COOK
And guardian was a host of Frankish spears;
So that the very porters did us reverence,
And fierce magicians skipped to open doors.
Sire Orobas, could I but write a gest
To tell my people of our wanderings,
Blind Homer would arise from out his grave;
Borrow, in heaven, would bless his very soul,
And Marco Polo, Huc, and Mungo Park
Would go out of the business. But, alas!
It may not be, for I am weak in cunning.
But, Orobas, when you and I become
Sad, toiling leeches in some noisome slum
And persons and events give us despite,
We still shall hold remembrance of these things —
How you and I were vagabond princes, once. . . .'

I·SEE·MY·YOUNG·COUNTRY-
MEN·DANCING·

52

7

'After such knowledge, what forgiveness?' asked Mr Eliot in 'Gerontion'. It was, I think, the main question which concerned Dr Mavor as he came to terms with the life of a general practitioner on the south side of Glasgow, a toiling leech in noisome slums, hospitals and — because he needed the money — a tobacco factory. It was the question which continued to gnaw at Mr Bridie and vibrated through many of the plays which he was soon to begin to write.

The Vagabond Prince returned to Glasgow and set about earning a living:

> In the autumn of 1919 I bought a practice in the Langside district of Glasgow and joined the staff of the Victoria Infirmary as a junior assistant physician. My mother, my brother, Eric, and I took up housekeeping in a little semi-villa with a garden in Langside Avenue. I began for the first time to do an honest day's work. In one way I regretted that I had left my protracted youth behind me. In another way I was glad. . . .
>
> I did not like being a general practitioner though the life had its compensations. I was conscious that I was learning a good deal. I learned how to talk to people and improved somewhat my technique in lying. I learned a little about human nature. I learned almost to a hair how much humbug is contained in the physician's alloy. I learned that, in women especially, invalidism is not so much an affliction as a powerful weapon. I learned that a doctor, unless he takes morphia, cannot starve. My practice grew steadily without any particular effort on my part. . . .
>
> It was pleasant to learn these things, but I did not look

forward with any pleasure to a continuance of my state. I was restless and discontented. I hunted continually for a way out. I had thought no small beer of myself as an author. I wrote a great deal in the hope that I should be paid for it and gather sufficient money to subsidise a consulting practice. I earned, by my typewriter, something like seven pounds in three years. . . .

He did, however, emancipate himself into consulting practice. He got his own wards in Stobhill Hospital, for which, unlike his position at the Victoria Infirmary, he was paid a decent salary. He became a Professor of Medicine at the Anderson's College, which was an extra-mural School of Medicine with a respectable reputation — David Livingstone was a graduate. He got an M.D. with commendation at Glasgow University. Alec Glen asks:

What kind of doctor was he? He prided himself in belonging to the old school of Glasgow clinicians. He was resident physician in the Royal Infirmary to W. R. Jack whom Mavor himself described as 'the last apostle in the line of Gairdner'. Most of the Glasgow teaching, however, at that time followed that tradition. We were taught to look on patients as individuals and treat them as such. Mavor examined the patient first and then looked at the X-ray afterwards, if he looked at it at all. Mrs Brown herself was more important to him than the X-ray plate or the laboratory diagnosis and he treated Mrs Brown in his own way. His patients all liked and trusted him. He had a very light and gentle touch with his fingers and was a real expert at the clinical examination of the heart and lungs. . . .

In 1934 there was a vacancy for a senior physician at the Victoria. Mavor had already been a senior physician [having returned to his old hospital] for several years. His side room was a rallying point for the staff. We went there when we were feeling a bit depressed and wanted to be cheered up. We went there when we were taking things too seriously and needed a proper perspective. We went there when anything happened to see what Mavor thought about it.

When Mavor heard that two of the senior physicians had applied for the vacancy he resigned himself from the staff to make room for both. None of us wanted him to retire and when he saw that I was a bit distressed about it he actually apologised to me for not retiring sooner.

Was it wise that he should have retired from his medical work at that time? I have often thought about it and I am still not sure. It is true that he had been living an extraordinarily busy life . . . [but] his contact with people was his main inspiration. He would never have been the great dramatist that he was if he had sat at his desk all his life in the country making up imaginary plays about imaginary people in imaginary situations. He now retired from all his medical appointments and moved out to Drymen where he lived among beautiful surroundings. He had a secretary. His output of plays and books continued high but not any higher, I believe, than during his medical career.

But this is to anticipate. In the middle of his building a medical career and before he became a writer he married Rona Bremner in June 1923.

Rona Bremner's family had, also, Free Church associations. Her grandfather Robert Bremner was the minister of the Gorbals Free Church. I briefly inherited a partner's desk, an immense oak construction, which I passed on to our village schoolmaster in Peeblesshire. It had a little silver plaque recording that it had been presented by the grateful ladies of the Rev. Bremner's congregation on his jubilee in the parish.

Robert Locke Bremner — the Lockes had been rather grand in Dumfries — was a Glasgow lawyer. He was busy with good works and, like Harry Mavor, something of a free thinker in those confused days at the turn of the century. Like the Mavors', the Bremners' house was Arts and Crafts in its decor and encouraged intellectual conversation. Mr Bremner ran several series of lectures in Glasgow and invited the giants of his day. He also travelled in Iceland and made some translations of the sagas.

His portrait shows a gentle, quiet man in a flat cap and Norfolk jacket. Clearly a son of the manse, he emancipated himself from his father's religion and evolved, in a sensible book, a workable religion of his own, embracing Darwin and the advances of science, coupled with his own strong feeling for social improvement. He was an early meliorist.

His wife, Christina, though I never heard her addressed as

O. H. Mavor and Rona Bremner on their wedding day, 1923. Photograph by T. & R. Annan, Glasgow.

anything but Mrs Bremner, was a Highland lady, from near Beauly on the Moray Firth, very beautiful in youth, with a splendid head and neck. Her, I knew very well, but not my grandfather. Rona was born in 1897, and was thus nearly ten years younger than Osborne Mavor. Her younger sister, Ailsa, was born in 1900.

Ailsa, who was a talented musician, was full of life and jollity, very fond of animals and, as an excellent pianist, much in demand in all kinds of circles. She certainly had more than one proposal of marriage, but she remained single and looked after Mrs Bremner for the rest of her life. 'Looked after' is not the right phrase: they lived very happily together in the bein village of Killearn, seventeen miles north of Glasgow, for forty years, and Ailsa, I'm sure, seldom or never regretted her choice. She had a full life and lived, until a couple of hypothermic episodes and Alzheimer's disease rendered her unable to look after herself, in the village, supported latterly by helpful neighbours. The Bremners' house, Achadhu, was really home to my brother and myself during our childhood, as Rona and Osborne began early, and continued, a wildly peripatetic lifestyle which took them through ten or so houses in their less than thirty years of married life. Achadhu was a nice house with a large garden, with hens and dogs and cats. Killearn did not get the electric light until I was old enough to remember, as the happiest symbol of my childhood, Mrs Bremner going round the house in the dusk, the fires flickering in the grates, collecting the tall lamps, cleaning their funnels and charging the bowls with methylated spirits, whistling tunelessly under her breath, then carrying the new, bright, glowing flames about the house — a ritual that involved basic things like light and shelter, but also the agreeable, untidy overspill of primitive technology, sounds and smells as well. Modern central heating is just fine: but what can replace the fall of a coal and the little yellow spurt of flame, casting sudden bright shadows on the walls?

Rona Mavor was, like her mother, something of a beauty. She had known Osborne, as the Bremners had known the Mavors, since early childhood, but during the War he had been engaged to a nurse, known as Geo, whom, however, the vagaries of the times drew from him. When Rona and Osborne met again he pursued a diligent courtship involving long midnight journeys by tram-car from Langside to Kelvinside. They were married in June 1923 and had two sons, my brother Robert and me, in the succeeding years.

I think that everyone who knew Rona during her married life enjoyed her company. She was a passable painter and had a real sensitivity to colour which she deployed in the decoration of her long succession of houses. She was an excellent hostess and a good manager: she paid all the bills, invested discreetly on the side, bought for a song some paintings which were a joy to look at and multiplied in value. Alas, most of her considerable energy was devoted to an anxiety which focused on her health. The cream of the medical profession failed to dislodge her from her large repertoire of symptoms, each of which she believed to herald some fatal illness, and all of which she survived to the age of eighty-nine.

Bridie's correspondence, notably that with Alastair and Naomi Sim, is shot through with regrets that Rona's current illness — asthma, or colitis, or neuritis, or whatever — makes it impossible to do this, that and the other; and I recollect many first nights when Osborne would go round to thank the actors and actresses and Rona, wheezing loudly, would stand impatient at the Stage Door, whispering that she *must* get home quickly for a cup of tea. This was very sad and I find it difficult to adopt a proper perspective on it, as I had, after my father's death, a further thirty-five years of inviting physicians, now my senior colleagues, as they had been my father's, to treat Rona. I think one of the reasons why they did not succeed was that she began, the moment she thought the doctor worthy of her, to enchant him with conversation, reminiscence and dry sherry. She was flirtatious and very fond of men — generally disliking women — but if a whisper of sex ever reared its ugly head (and I do not suggest that it ever did in the respectable encounters with the Scottish medical profession) she would be shocked and rapidly retreat.

When my father died she had, oddly, a brief period of excellent health and was invited to join several Boards: the Citizens' Theatre, the Broadcasting Council for Scotland, the Scottish Arts Council. At that time I left my job at the American Hospital of Paris to be with her. When I moved to a hospital in Glasgow her illnesses returned.

As a member of the Broadcasting Council she once hosted a dinner party for a Brains Trust programme and, at a lateish hour, posed for them the question whether it was not Love but Jealousy which made the world go round. After a rather *mauvais quart d'heure* of sticky conversation Hector McNeil, then Foreign Secretary, said that, in his view, it was Fear which was the motivating force, at least in international affairs. Rona wrote to me some time later saying that a cloud had passed over my face when she posed her question. I'm sure it did: it was at once an insightful and an alarmingly naïve thing to say. She *was* jealous and possessive in a way that did no good to her or to her husband. And yet I think it was, in many ways, a happy marriage. Friends remember what fun they had in Rona's succession of houses. She, shortly after my father died, wrote to a friend that what she most missed was *his* fun which went on all day.

If her illnesses were, to some extent, her most powerful weapon, she confessed to Naomi Sim that, though she felt terribly guilty at having been such a nuisance to Osborne (and she never achieved the insight to believe her illnesses psychogenic), she had, perhaps, stimulated him to the remarkable feat of writing nearly forty plays in twenty years. When Rona was ill he did not go out, or away: he went to his typewriter and wrote. There is truth in this.

If I have been unfair — after the thirty-five years since my father's death — I ask forgiveness from the shades of both my parents. And I may well be wrong. Virtually all Osborne's friends regarded him as a happy man. I thought he was probably *not* happy. He had returned from his adventurous youth and married, and he took on the duties of domesticity and fulfilled them *sans peur* and *sans reproche*. It was what his Glasgow bourgeois upbringing, the *mores* inculcated in him by his parents, demanded.

It is possible that his art suffered. But, whatever may be thought nowadays, Dr Mavor and Mr Bridie agreed, at the end of the day, that it was better to be a good man than a good artist should the two callings prove mutually exclusive.

8

One Way of Living has the following Imaginary Conversation in Heaven:

> Oliver Goldsmith sat down beside me. 'You are about, I judge, to tell us how you came to be a writer of stage plays. That will interest me. I have been confused somewhat by the stories told me by Schiller, Chekhov, Schnitzler and Maugham. My own motives were, I confess, less complicated than theirs. I have always attributed this vice of mine to unsuitable company and the immoderate use of wine and spirits. With these others there appears to have been an element of paranoid dementia — of the hearing of voices.'
> 'Indeed, Doctor,' I replied, 'I am afraid you will find little satisfaction to your curiosity in anything I am about to write on the intermediate steps between Doctor and Dramatist. I am inclined to put it down to sheer laziness.'

In many later articles Mr Bridie was inclined to refer to a Law of Compensation whereby the bloodiest detective novels were written by gentle, spinster ladies, and novels about politics and the fall of empires by reclusive village-dwellers. No one, he often said, would *write* about life who had any talent for living it. In a letter he wrote in 1930 he proposed:

> Now the only common factor artists have is a faculty for translating emotion into concrete terms. . . . Take them individually and in the lump they have defects to set against this faculty — moral, social, commercial and intellectual defects. I think myself, the intellectual defects are the most

outstanding and the least realised by the artists themselves. They cannot conceive how a person gifted by the Almighty with Vision should be unable to integrate the details of *this* Vision right and left and all over the place. Hence the screaming, hysterical imbecilities you can hear from very competent painters. . . .

My favourite text on the transition from ordinary chap to writer comes from Proust. It is from *A l'ombre des jeunes filles en fleurs*, my own translation:

> But genius, even substantial talent, springs less from intellectual elements or from a superior degree of social sensitivity than other people possess, rather from the faculty of being able to transform them, transpose them. To warm a saucepan with an electric light bulb you don't need the brightest possible lamp, but one that ceases to give out light and converts its current into heat instead. To fly you don't need the most powerful automobile, but a machine which, ceasing to go along the road, projects a line at right angles to the one it's going along, and converts its horizontal speed into a vertical lifting force. In the same way, those who produce works of genius are not those who live in the most delicate atmosphere, who make the most brilliant conversation, have the widest culture; but those who, brusquely ceasing to live their own lives, are able to make their personalities into a sort of mirror in which these lives, however dull and unimportant they may be in a worldly, or even, to some extent, intellectual sense, are reflected, the genius consisting in the reflecting power and not in the intrinsic quality of whatever is reflected. The day that the young Bergotte was able to show to his readers the tasteless household in which he had spent his childhood and the not particularly interesting conversations he had with his brothers, that day he surpassed the wittier and more distinguished friends of his family: they could go home in their Rolls-Royces sneering a bit at the vulgarity of the Bergottes; but he, his rather modest machine having at last taken off, he soared above them.

I suspect it was in some such way that the doctor became the writer. On the surface the transition was rapid and easy. Below the surface it was complex and difficult.

In his university days, Osborne Mavor had written at least five plays for student performance. They were called: *The Son who was considerate of his Father's Prejudices, No Wedding Cake for Her, The Duke who could sometimes hardly keep from Smiling, Ethics Among Thieves,* and *The Baron who would not be convinced that his Way of Living was anything out of the Ordinary.* To this list Professor Renwick, a university friend and Professor of English at Edinburgh, added *The Duke Who Sometimes Smiled,* which sounds very like number three, above, and *The Young Man to whom Romance was as the Bread of his Being,* which, with all respect to the distinguished Professor, I suspect was called *The Young Man to whom Romance was as the Breath of his Being,* but I have not seen a copy, although Renwick records that one survived. It was written in 1912.

A major influence in university days was Alfred Wareing, who ran the Glasgow Repertory Theatre and, as we have seen, went camping in Arran. Osborne Mavor's first full-length play, written after he returned from the wars, was *The Switchback,* which he sent to Wareing who said it was very clever, but that no manager would risk a brace button on it.

A second influence was Dr MacIntyre, a general practitioner, author of a number of decent plays published under the name of John Brandane, a skilled play-doctor, and a pillar of the Scottish National Players. The Scottish National Players were a remarkable group of actors sponsored by the St Andrew's Society of Glasgow, and inspired by the achievements of the Abbey Theatre in Dublin and the whole movement which began in the late 1880s with Antoine's *Théâtre Libre* in Paris and had been forwarded by the remarkable Miss Horniman who, finally disenchanted with the Abbey and the Irish, founded in Manchester the first of the great and continuing chain of civic theatres, of which Alfred Wareing's Glasgow Repertory Theatre was, I think, the third.

The actors of the Scottish National Players were, technically, amateurs, but they rehearsed for long hours, evening after evening, and they hired a professional producer, or, as we would now say, director. At the time the young Tyrone Guthrie:

A young professional producer had just been engaged. He had been trained with J.B.Fagan's Oxford Players, and had been with the B.B.C. at Belfast. He was an Irishman of

Scottish extraction, born at Tunbridge Wells and educated at Wellington and St John's, Oxford. He was six feet four high and wore a jersey and sandals. Brandane did not entirely approve of him. He had a friend called David Cleghorn Thomson, who was Regional Director for Scotland of the B.B.C. The ideas of these two gentlemen did not conform strictly to the canon laid down by the St Andrew's Society of Glasgow.

It is perhaps proper to note that the ideas of these two gentlemen, to which the St Andrew's Society took exception, found their expression in silk dragon dressing-gowns and Turkish cigarettes in long holders. Mavor records: 'His [Guthrie's] predilections at this time ran somewhat in the direction of song, mime and step-ladders; and Brandane, Bottomley and Walter Buchanan of the St Andrew's Society regarded these things as dangerous innovations', and adds, 'I think rightly'.

I was elected to the Board. The battle was not so bitter as John Brandane's Highland and bloody imagination had pictured it, although we recruited a red-headed, fiery specialist in diseases of children who had dandled David Thomson on his knee and was not prepared to stand any nonsense from him. My first step towards compromise was to write a play with almost everything in it but step-ladders. It was called *The Sunlight Sonata, or To Meet The Seven Deadly Sins.* Guthrie liked it. With magnificent courtesy and patience he helped me to iron out its amateur crudities. Brandane liked it, because, although it leaned over to the fantastic, it was as Scots as Freuchie. The Devil spoke from the top of Ben Lomond, addressing the Seven Deadly Sins in braid Scots hexameters, and the eight of them interfered in the private lives of a bunch of quite justly observed Glasgow citizens picnicking on the Bonnie Banks. Three pantomime fairies called Faith, Hope and Charity, intervened. It was the last and only survivor of my morality play period, and I thought it very amusing. I wrote it on a Sunday and had to ring up a clergyman of my acquaintance to find out exactly who the Seven Deadly Sins were. He did not know.

The Sunlight Sonata was first performed at the Lyric Theatre in Glasgow on 20th March 1928. Methuen had published *Some*

Talk of Alexander in 1926, the memoirs of Baku and all that. Dr Mavor had then adopted the pseudonym of James Bridie. The play, however, was described as being by Mary Henderson, which led to some confusion. From now on, though, it was Bridie all the way.

Brandane worked with him on *The Switchback* and suggested he send it to Sir Barry Jackson, the impresario of the Birmingham Repertory Theatre. It was performed there a year after *The Sunlight Sonata*. Jackson presented *What it is to be Young*, not a very good play, in November 1929. In July of 1930 the Masque Theatre Company played *The Anatomist* in Edinburgh.

> In the middle of the week before we opened I got a panic-stricken message from Gurney [the producer] that he could not make head or tail of my script. I went through to Edinburgh and found that, indeed, the script did not seem to have much sense in it. I did not recognise it as my own, and we turned the Lyceum Theatre upside down looking for the original manuscript. We found it at last below a pile of press cuttings. Some person or persons unknown had been doodling over it with a blue pencil, and the typist had done her best. The unfortunate actors set themselves straight away to commit the more intelligible version to memory, and at a quarter to eight on Monday night the curtain went up five minutes after the dress rehearsal had stopped.
>
> The actor who played the leading part forgot altogether the two sets of words he had learned, but carried through the part with great verve by dint of shouting 'God Almighty!', 'Damn!', 'Rot their souls!' and 'Barbara Celarent!' at suitable intervals. His interlocutors gave him as many of his words as they could remember, but, as he was a little deaf, they very often had to speak the words themselves, prefacing them with 'As you very truly observe' or 'As you are never tired of remarking', or some such appropriate phrase. The performance was a great success and the dramatic critics of Edinburgh said that the first great Scottish play had yet to be written. One of them said, quite truly, that I had a great deal to learn of the elements of my craft.

In November 1930 the Scottish National Players performed a modest comedy called *The Girl who did not want to go to Kuala*

Lumpur. Tyrone Guthrie had moved from Glasgow to Cambridge where he was directing the Festival Theatre under the remarkable manager, Anmer Hall. In the same month he played the Angel Raphael, in Bridie's *Tobias and the Angel*, directed by Evan John.

The following year Barry Jackson revived *The Switchback*, this time with Cedric Hardwicke in the lead, for the important Malvern Festival; and Anmer Hall opened a new theatre in London, the Westminster, with *The Anatomist*, directed by Guthrie and with Henry Ainley as Dr Knox. It was followed, in March 1932, by *Tobias and the Angel*, with Ainley as Raphael and directed by Guthrie. It was a very promising start for a middle-aged dramatist.

But Dr Mavor had written to Alfred Wareing on 17th January 1931:

> I wouldn't mind so much if my so-called Consulting Practice had not entirely disappeared. I am now definitely known as a bloody fool who writes plays and the fact that I spend all day and every day learning how to heal the sick and that I know my job better than 90% of my colleagues (golfers to a man) is of none effect. So as far as I can see I have got to hit up some siller to pay my debts by writing for the theatre, tho' God knows it is more respectable to be a pianist in a brothel. . . .
>
> Now, Alfred, rally round with the wise counsel. If by wagging your frosty pow you can save my wife and innocent children from a pauper's crust, I am sure you will.

And, on 9th August 1932, after the substantial success of *The Anatomist*, and the more modest run of *Tobias and the Angel*, which has since proved by far his most frequently performed play, he wrote again:

> Here am I with the dramatic critics from The Observer to Reynolds, from Shaw to Swaffer saying I have the goods. I have a page in the newest history of the British Drama. In the year 1931-32 I took all the money that was made in a one-horse little high-brow theatre at the back of H.M. Stables, and (with the assistance of Mr Ainley) put it and its producer and its scenic artist and its best actress [Flora Robson in *The Anatomist*] right on the map. Why am I not on the map myself? Managements are howling to the moon

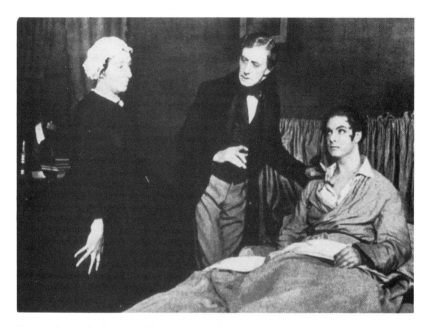

Scene from A *Sleeping Clergyman* with Beatrix Feilden-Kaye, Ernest Thesiger, and Robert Donat. Reproduced from the *Illustrated London News*, 7 October 1933.

for plays and I assure you I am treated by them as if I were Miss Menopause of Bournemouth sending in a little masque for children. . . .

But there, there, there. Should I go to London and invest £100 in a party to a Lord or two and have it reported in the Tatler? Should I write a bit of smart bawdry that would bring Agate and Ivor Brown and Morgan heavily down on me? Or should I chuck the business altogether? It just saved me from bankruptcy and finally ruined my consulting practice last year, but I could live without it. Or if the best method is to throw one'sself on the mercy of the mistresses and young gentlemen friends of the MANAGERS, who are they and how are they to be approached?

Take your time, laddie. Write on one side of the paper.

A couple of years earlier he had written, it would seem in a similar mood, to Sir Barry Jackson, who replied, on 2nd April 1930:

It is too bad of you to throw the onus of your future career on my shoulders. I might say 'Throw up your work for the theatre', in which case I should probably be depriving posterity of a genius; and on the other hand, by advising you to give up your medical work I might be responsible for your starvation. Frankly I think you have undeniable gifts for dramatic work, but to me, there are obvious symptoms of haste, or lack of time in the carrying out. I was aware of this in 'Tobit' [sic] as in the other plays, and I doubt very much whether this work would get further than Birmingham as it stands.

No doubt all the foregoing is disappointing, for I believe really that your heart is in the theatre; but I can only advise you, as I have advised many others, that 'safety' is a good game to play, and safety in the theatre simply does not exist.

Dr Mavor did not take Sir Barry's advice. In July 1933 Shaw's new play was not ready for the Malvern Festival and Jackson produced Bridie's *A Sleeping Clergyman*, with Robert Donat in the lead, instead.

9

The earliest plays were written at 17 Fitzroy Place, a grimy westward extension of Sauchiehall Street. The front door was approached by six or seven steps, and next to it was a similar door giving entry to the flats upstairs. The house itself had its front windows on both sides of the doors: it wrapped itself round the ascending stairway, so that footsteps rising and falling sounded through the whole house and at all hours. The front rooms were my father's Consulting Room and the Drawing Room. At the back were a bedroom, a dining room and the nursery. Half way along the corridor leading to the nursery was a stair descending to the kitchen and the maids' quarters, below ground level. There was a small overgrown garden, beyond which was a lane, and beyond that Argyle Street, *terra incognita* to my brother and myself. We were on the very borders of gentility. We were, however, only a hundred yards from the West End Park where we were taken for walks and where I learnt, through a series of alarming falls, to ride a bicycle. We splashed in the fountain and fed the ducks.

The Mavors were hard up in the Fitzroy Place days. I understand that at a certain point Uncle Sam's chauffeur handed in a small package. It was a hundred pounds with a note from Sam to say that he had found this lying about the house and, having no use for it, would be grateful if Rona and Osborne would accept it as a gift.

Of course propriety demanded that a consulting physician have a housemaid, but I rather think that at that stage the cook had to double as a door-opener and table-maid. There was also a nanny or governess to take us to the park, but only for an hour or two in the afternoons. Somehow I never seem to remember my mother as participating in these excursions: but it is possible that, as I was an exceptionally unobservant child, I simply failed to recognise her. We left 17 Fitzroy Place three months after my fifth birthday, and my memories of the house, in spite of the fact that it has since become a bookshop and I revisited it some years ago, are few and unclear.

My father's Consulting Room I don't remember at all. It was a door, off the hall, that was shut and that guarded certain mysteries. The nursery had a blue carpet with a white surround which, miraculously, one year became a white carpet with a blue surround. I slept there in a cot and watched the flickering patterns of the coal fire on the ceiling. I remember the poet Gordon Bottomley — a late Georgian — dominating the drawing-room and using his left hand, held horizontally, to keep his walrus moustache from plunging into his tea. I remember being ill — tonsillitis, I suspect — and spending long nights gazing at an *art nouveau* jar with an owl on it. I remember a strawberry cake in the cake shop on the corner — on the way to the Park — that I always desired but never tasted. I remember a Punch and Judy show. And I remember Osborne on, it must have been, April 1st 1929 or 1930, telling me, in the drawing-room, to go and fetch Aunt Ailsa and my brother Robert to come and see the soldiers. In those days soldiers marching past were an exciting entertainment. I can still see them rushing in in eager anticipation, and he had two lead toy soldiers which he diddled on the back of an armchair. I thought it a highly disreputable trick and, I think, still do so and am unhappy about it, though I doubt that either Ailsa or Robert thought it other than a witty April Fool's Day joke.

Gordon Bottomley must have written to the emerging playwright, praising the recently published *The Switchback* and two other plays and comparing some of the work to Chekhov. His letter brought the following reply on 10th April 1930:

> I wonder if you realise what heady stuff your vintage Burgundy is. I am back in the days when I, a rabbit of the rabbits, began suddenly to hit sixes from first class bowling — and then woke up. Or I am like the mouse in the story who, after three drops of ——'s Highland Liqueur, flicked his whiskers & went hunting for the cat. In an obscure corner of John O'London's Weekly I am compared with those ill-assorted Scots, Barrie and Burns. Neil Gunn, the Exciseman, sends

me Pre-War Over-Proof Vatted Pot Still Glenlivet, saying I am like Arthur Balfour and what not. And George Blake in the Northern Edition of the Daily Express says, 'Scotland has found a Shaw; no more and no less than that.' I have a good head for whisky; it only makes me melancholy; but you are in another cellar, and Tchekhov is out of the cat and into the tiger class. However — it is tremendously exhilarating & what care I? The millionaires can keep their vulgar fizzy drinks. . . .

With the passage in your letter in which you say that the reflex of a situation is the proper material for a play, I must agree. It's much more flexible material under the limitations of stage production. But I'm trying to avoid forming any theories about play-writing at all. I honestly find brute stupidity and ignorance an asset in this business. I prefer to go mad for a little, keeping a sharp lookout for absurdities as they arise, but having no fixed conscious criterion of self-criticism. This half-witted method has this practical advantage that it has brought me your good opinion; and I value that.

The cricketing image is not a metaphor. He was not to hit sixes from the best bowling in the theatre for a year or two yet, with *The Anatomist* and *Tobias and the Angel* at the Westminster. At this point Dr Mavor had written two plays, *The Switchback* and *What it is to be Young*, which had been performed at the Birmingham Repertory Theatre, and a couple for the Scottish National Players. Constable had, in those good days, bravely published *The Switchback* and *The Sunlight Sonata* with an adaptation of Chaucer's *The Pardoner's Tale*. He was writing *The Anatomist* and *Tobias and the Angel*.

He was just over forty, the most difficult age. He had survived the War and had the beginnings of a consulting practice, a wife and two small children, but he was changing the direction of his energies. He was going to be a playwright: and he moved house.

In October 1930 we moved across the West End Park and up to the gallant terraces surrounding Park Circus. Number 6 Woodlands Terrace stood four storeys high, looked for miles across the river to the South — on a clear day you could see the peaks of Arran — and at the end of the terrace there was, and happily still is, a noble group of high pencil-like towers, a miniature San Gimigniano, dominating the West End of Glasgow. The move to Woodlands Terrace is described thus in *One Way of Living*:

I had . . . some little difficulty in paying my grocer's bill. I solved the problem of the grocer's bill by carrying out one of the few really brilliant ideas of my life. I bought a new house. I recommend this to anybody finding himself financially in a tight corner. A building society paid for the house, the bank furnished it and I lived on the proceeds of these crazy transactions for nearly a year.

It was the first house in which my mother was able to indulge her talent for interior decoration, presumably thanks to the bank. The grey staircase carpet was held in place by red, blue, yellow and green carpet rods. The dining-room was gold with, I think, red curtains, the drawing-room pale apple green. As the move was in October 1930 and the letters to Alfred Wareing, quoted in the last chapter, are of January 1931 and August 1932, the grandeur of Woodlands Terrace must have been enjoyed somewhat tentatively at best, at least to begin with.

I am told that I sleep-walked — for the first and last time in my life — early after our occupancy, being found not in the bedroom which Robert and I shared on the first floor — a thin room in which our beds were foot to foot and a tall window looked out on an owl-haunted tree in the drab back-garden — but in the middle of the nursery on the top floor. Robert continued as a compulsive bed-wetter and Rona was frequently unwell. But I remember rather grand dinner parties (with a little machine for making-your-own-pink-ice-cream) and a gathering of the Music Club at which Ailsa was to play.

Dr Mavor's last consulting room was again first on the right off the hall. I remember this one rather well. It had very tall bookcases full of musty books, and an examination couch that folded up and down in all sorts of entertaining ways. It was made of ebony and bamboo wickerwork: this was long before stainless steel and rubber. There was a microscope and a little cupboard full of disinfectant smells. For the greatest Christmas that ever was — and I think it was 1931 — all the presents were secreted in the consulting room and on that astonishing morning there was a pile for Robert on one chair, a pile for me on the other, and an even bigger pile for both of us on the examination couch: so if there was a problem with poverty it was mitigated poverty.

At first Robert and I walked, as I have said, through the

Scene from the first London performance of *The Anatomist* with Robert Eddison, Henry Ainley and Carleton Hobbs, 1931. Photograph by Sasha.

Park and the railway station to the Academy, but a Harley Street consultant to whom he was taken on a visit to London — I think it would be 1932 — recommended that he be sent away to school: so we were both packed off to Belmont House as weekly boarders, returning most weekends. The school was just across town, in Newton Mearns, and was run by a slightly eccentric enthusiast who later took orders in the Episcopal Church. I guess it was like most preparatory schools from Kipling to Evelyn Waugh. I was cast as Scrubbins, a small boy, in a Mock Trial the day Noel Coward came to lunch, sweeping round the corner of Woodlands Terrace in an amazing toffee-coloured drop-head Rolls-Royce. He advised me to 'burst into tears and throw myself on the mercy of the Court'. But that must have been later. . . .

Before, and during, the move Mr Bridie had been busy. He

had written *The Anatomist* and *Tobias and the Angel*, the two plays which established his reputation when they were performed in London in 1932. The first, as we have seen, had been a near disaster in Edinburgh, the latter a success at the Cambridge theatre with Guthrie as the Angel. A play that is going to make one's reputation is, however, fairy gold when it has been performed only for a couple of weeks in a provincial theatre. How did Dr Mavor feel about Mr Bridie's potential? I am no witness in this case. I remember Osborne once taking us for a walk — I'm sure as the result of many complaints from Rona. It was a strange experience for us. I remember wondering who was this man and why was he taking us for a walk. I remember he said we would go on a Mystery Tour and take the first street on the left, the second on the right and so on. . . . It was clearly a new experience for both parties. I think he did well, but he didn't have a natural liking for children although he was not averse to games. He used to invent war games with hills and roads and soldiers constructed on a rug in the spare bedroom: one cast dice and made moves. I think he enjoyed them. I don't think I did much. Robert probably did. And he painted scenery and characters for a toy theatre which, again, I'm not sure I was as enchanted with as I should have been.

But what was going on in that other world, the creative mind of Mr Bridie?

It seems clear that, as Sir Barry Jackson had observed, 'his heart was in the theatre'. More than that, he had the torturing thought that 'he had yet to speak on God's behalf'. But he was a middle-aged Glasgow physician with a wife and two children, thirled to the *mores* of his Glasgow bourgeois society. The early plays, then, wrestle with that predicament. Their protagonists share, in one sense or another, the confinements of the chrysalis Dr Mavor, not yet sure of his butterfly talents as Mr Bridie.

The hero of *The Switchback*, potent title, Dr Mallaby, believes he has discovered a cure — or rather a vaccine — for tuberculosis. He is tempted, encouraged by his wife, to publish too early. He makes a grab at fame and fortune, but the discovery is flawed. He is rejected by the medical establishment and by the media. Half-mad but undefeated he sets out for Palmyra and 'the desiccated wisdom lying silent under the sands'.

Eternal towers! O Memphis, Mycenae, Babylon, Thebes!

Carthage, Nineveh, Tyre! Issos, Shusa, Palmyra! Jackals howl there and the dust blows there, and the clever ones and all they did are nothing and less than nothing. O cities, I'll go to you. I'll fill my soul with you! You know, you cities, how soon, in how little time our shoddy little concrete and stucco world will be bitten to death by bacteria, shrouded in jungle and burnt there by the sun. . . .

I'll go to Palmyra. There's a place! All the groves and fountains and clever ones disputing about the best advice to give to the Almighty.

The mosquitoes bred in their lily pools and bit malaria into their blood. And their glossy skins yellowed and dried and their eyes grew dull and their brains shrivelled and their spleens grew and their palaces and their cisterns crumbled away. And their laws and opinions and pronouncements and edicts and discoveries were lost among the thin air.

This is not your average new author describing his first sexual experience in Hemingwayan short jabs. And he had *been* to Palmyra. Unlike Dr Mallaby, his problem was not how to break away, but how to settle down.

Dr Knox, in *The Anatomist*, is an historical figure who came to grief over his association with the murderers and body-snatchers Burke and Hare. Finding a source of income in supplying the Anatomy Department, they facilitated the supply of fresh corpses by a little murder on the side. Bridie's Knox is, on any careful reading of the play, fully aware of this, yet he protests the 'greater good' of his pursuit of the science of anatomy. 'Do you think because I strut and rant and put on a bold face that my soul isn't sick within me at the horror of what I have done?' he asks his lady friend Amelia. And yet Bridie does not ask us to condemn him. He is left at the end of the play lecturing brilliantly, his students 'listening with passionate intentness', and claiming that although he carries 'the deaths of those poor wretches round my neck till I die. And perhaps after that . . . the cause is between Robert Knox and Almighty God'.

What does this mean? It becomes the central topic of most of Bridie's early plays. There is a protagonist who believes that he 'speaks on God's behalf' and that, therefore, he must be given some sort of leave to extend the limits which are properly set upon the behaviour of his associates. The rather minor play he wrote for the Scottish National Players (performed February 1931), *The Dancing Bear*, has the same theme. The local poet is engaged to marry Miss Murdoch and money, but he has more fellow-feeling for Jean, the maid:

> JEAN: Do ye no' want to get married to Miss Murdoch?
> COLIN: I do not, and that's a fact.
> JEAN: Oh!
> COLIN: This is the first time I've admitted it, even to myself. I've maybe no' seen the next ten years clearly till this minute. Maybe I've held my e'en awa from those ten years in case I couldna abide them. Oh, Jean, I'm in for it. I'm in for a living hell . . . Jean . . . Ye've heard of Shelley . . . and Byron . . . and Burns? Well . . . I'm made like them in a way. I canna write like them, if ye understand me, but some way I've gotten a twist they a' had.

So he deserts Miss Murdoch and runs off with Jean.

In *Tobias and the Angel*, Raphael, having conducted little Tobias on his journey and given him a wife and modest prosperity, rebukes Sara when she finds herself falling in love, not with her husband, but with his 'daemon':

> RAPHAEL: You may fall in love with a man's daemon — indeed it is advisable and stimulating to do so, provided that, at the back of your mind, you remember that you are only falling in love in a Pickwickian sense.
> SARA: I don't understand you.
> RAPHAEL: I shall try to make myself clear. A daemon, spelt with an 'a', is a creature by whose agency you write immortal verse, go great journeys, leap into bottomless chasms, fight dragons, starve in a garret . . .
> SARA: Strangle your husbands.
> RAPHAEL: Yes. That too. . . . Foolish women, of whom you are one, fall in love with daemons. Your excuse has been that a daemon of the inferior sort has tormented you since you were a child. He made you impatient with common men. . . . You must cease to be so. Often, at odd times in the future, you will see me looking out of Tobias's eyes. But you must look the other way and busy yourself with your household tasks.

For I have no pity for you.

You must study Tobias, and Tobias alone — his little oddities, his bursts of friendliness, his gentleness, his follies. You must love him for those and for his little fat body.

SARA: But how can I help loving his daemon?

RAPHAEL: You cannot love what you cannot understand. Love what you understand and you will understand more and more till your life is so full that there will be no room for anything else — torturings and itchings and ambitions and shames.

It is hard not to see Dr Mavor lecturing Mrs Mavor on the character of Mr Bridie, and warning her off. It is also hard not to suspect, here, the beginnings of a retreat into what R. D. Laing in his brilliant book on the schizoid personality, *The Divided Self*, called an 'inner self', which has to be protected from the experiences of the harsh world. The question was on what terms one who had 'not much liked being a general practitioner' might be able to be a writer. Though as yet unproved, he felt he had 'gotten a twist' that Shelley and Byron and Burns, significant choices, might have had.

His almost exact contemporaries Eugene O'Neill and T. S. Eliot were prepared to demand certain freedoms, at some cost to their wives and, in O'Neill's case, families. Dr Mavor was not so sure that the gift of Vision was a permit to push people about, or even to make them unhappy. And he had seen plenty of unhappiness.

Jonah and the Whale, of which he was to write four versions (so it was clearly of deep interest to him), is about a man who, indisputably — he had, after all, been swallowed by a whale and cast up on the shore — had the best possible evidence that God wished him to speak on His behalf. But Jonah's prophecy of the downfall of Nineveh just didn't come off. Was he mistaken? Or had God changed His mind? Or, terrible thought, may God have a sense of humour?

In his later plays Bridie moved on from this anxiety about the artist's predicament, but it remained a major theme. The artist is persuaded that he is about God's work, that God has whispered to him a certain truth, granted him a certain vision. What is the validity of that vision? And what licence has the artist to force it on others, on his society, on his family? It is the central question of many of Ibsen's plays from *Brand* to *When We Dead Awaken*.

On the public level things went well. *A Sleeping Clergyman* was the success of the Malvern Festival and transferred to the Piccadilly Theatre where it ran for nine months. While it was there his next play, *Marriage is no Joke*, opened at the Globe, almost next door, and closed after five nights.

Ralph Richardson played a Highland divinity student who has wild adventures in Persia and Junglipore, becoming, almost, the king of that country. At the end of the play he is a decent Glasgow minister of religion but his erstwhile lover, the astonishing Nastasya, turns up with a group of Cossack Dancers at the Palaceum Theatre. He is tempted to return to the excitements of the Middle East but decides that he should stay with his little wife, Priscilla, and his measles-smitten children. 'Here is life,' he says, if a little unconvincingly, at the end. It was to become the resolution of not a few Bridie plays from then on.

I think I could have wished that Mr Bridie had taken more note of this, his most disastrous failure in the theatre. In a deeply suspect exculpatory essay, published in the Library Edition of the plays, he complained that the audience had accepted his wild inventions of 'a Highland divinity student . . . making a beast of himself with rum; entering, under a cloud of alcoholic verbiage, into a frivolously undertaken marriage contract; committing a dangerous and brutal assault upon a servant; and, later, handing over the entire control of his destiny to a half-educated, underbred, little hussy of a wife'. The second part of the play, set in Persia, was, he said, on the other hand, totally based upon something that really happened, and written with the utmost restraint. The audience and the critics regarded it as pure melodrama.

The truth is that Macgregor is simply *not* so regarded by the audience — or, I believe, the author. Nor is his wife. What destroys the play is its sudden close: its sudden decision for domesticity and a foreclosing of the action to which Macgregor, shirtless and heroic, seemed drawn as a moth to the flame.

A Sleeping Clergyman, however, was a major critical success and not a few observed that the mantle of Shaw had fallen on Bridie's shoulders. In that play the hero, even if after a couple of generations, achieves his apotheosis.

Charles Cameron is a brilliant biochemist. He dies young but his fiancée bears his child who produces twins before murdering her lover and jumping over a cliff. The third generation, Hope and Charlie, redeem the family. Hope works at Geneva for an international organisation. Charlie finds a cure for a pandemic of influenza. Dr Marshall has fostered the three generations. God, in the person of an elderly clergyman, who sleeps throughout, fidgets occasionally in His sleep.

> MARSHALL: Yes. Charlie Cameron the First had the spark in his poor diseased body. Now lettest thou thy servant depart in peace. I did my best to keep the spark alive, and now it's a great flame in Charlie and you.
>
> HOPE: Oh, Uncle Will, I'm a barren old woman.
>
> MARSHALL: Charlie's your brother and your lover and your son. You will make him do great things for the world . . . if the world is worth it.
>
> HOPE: Whether the world is worth it or not.

This was a resolution apt to the story of the play, although we shall see that at an early stage the director and producer had doubts about it. The resolution of *Marriage is no Joke*, opting for domesticity, rang false. I believe that this was not a matter of technical skill or immaturity. The creative mind of Mr Bridie still inhabited the body — and mind — of Dr Mavor, an admirable person. He continued to face the problem of how far to release the sleeping dragons of that creative mind. The child of his heredity, the pupil of his experience, he was not prepared to let them roam free.

10

In February 1934 Mr Bridie rushed back to Glasgow from the unhappy First Night of *Marriage is no Joke*, during the interval of which he had, however, hopped round the corner of Shaftesbury Avenue and been stayed with flagons by the company of *A Sleeping Clergyman*, which ran for nine months and was still at the Piccadilly. His presence, or that of Dr Mavor, was required because, at the age of nine, I was having an operation on my mastoid sinus.

A Sleeping Clergyman, although James Agate in the *Sunday Times* was confused by it, was, and was seen to be, a major play. Donat revived it many years later, with Margaret Lockwood, at the Criterion and, again, it proved a critical and public success. It was directed by H. K. Ayliff, who had directed *The Switchback* and was to direct five other Bridie plays. He had worked with Sir Barry Jackson at the Birmingham Repertory Theatre for over ten years, and continued to do so at successive Malvern Festivals. The name of Sir Barry Jackson is much better known than that of Ayliff, and Jackson was an exceptional impresario. He took risks and he paid the bills. The actual business of directing the plays and training the actors, however, was Ayliff's. In *One Way of Living*, Bridie wrote:

> This tall, cadaverous, ingenious man has never had his fair share of glory in the theatre. He does not go to parties, he never takes a curtain call, he does not make speeches at luncheons on the future of the theatre. Actors and actresses of the first rank who owe their early training to him seldom mention him. They like to think that they sprang fully armed from the forehead of Jove, or, at least that their genius grew

H. K. Ayliff. Photograph by Hugo. By permission of Malvern Festival Theatre.

from their early battles with misery and starvation. To remember the old school-master who taught them all they know blurs the beauty of these conceptions. In the early days, I am told, he had a tongue like a file, and this may explain why, from time to time, he has lacked advancement. Advancement or no advancement, he has cut his work deep in the history of the theatre and characteristically omitted to sign it.

I have noticed that, although he directed the first productions of *Back to Methuselah*, *Heartbreak House*, *The Apple Cart*, and *In Good King Charles's Golden Days*, to mention only four of the plays of Bernard Shaw, his name does not appear in St John Irvine's massive biography of Shaw. Bridie was always loyal to his old friends and teachers, and when Ayliff was in his late seventies and asked advice Bridie demurred, saying that he still regarded himself as 'Ayliff's novice'. After John Brandane, he regarded Ayliff as his teacher.

Their correspondence was, however, far from obsequious. As a Lowland Scot, Bridie liked nothing better than a good argument. And Ayliff always said what he thought. Both, too, liked jokes —

not anecdotes or gossip, but witty *aperçus*, arising from the context of the letter. Ayliff writes on February 9th, 1933, about Barry Jackson and the proposal to present *A Sleeping Clergyman* at Malvern:

> B.V.J. won't make up his mind till he's seen the end of the play. He murmured a bit about it being difficult to stage and I was annoying enough to be sure it was as easy as pie to do (and so it is; unless one was fool enough to ruin it with built-up sets). Anyway, please finish it — and carefully — as soon as you can and be sure to end up with a good grand finale. He's so pleased with my wise-crack about you and the sewing up of the body that he'll suspect your last scenes for ever and a day! It was careless of me.

Ayliff had remarked that Bridie was like a surgeon who, when he had removed the tumour, wandered out of the operating theatre, leaving his assistants to sew up the wound. It was a criticism that — Barry Jackson apart — was to haunt Bridie's dramaturgy for the rest of his life. The critics complained that his last acts, instead of resolving the problems and situations in the play, tended to be drafts of the *next* play he was going to write. His magnificent riposte, though I confess myself not entirely persuaded by it, was:

> And all this nonsense about last acts. Only God can write last acts, and He seldom does. You should go out of the theatre with your head whirling with speculations. You should be lovingly selecting infinite possibilities for the characters you have seen on the stage. What further interest for you have they, if they are neatly wrapped up and bedded or coffined? It makes me angry to hear these doctrinaire duds. . . .

As I suggested with *Marriage is no Joke,* Mr Bridie as critic is not always a reliable judge of Mr Bridie as playwright. And I believe that it was precisely when he *did* attempt to wrap his plays up neatly, to have his characters coffined and bedded, that he failed. In the late *Gog and Magog* the mad poet curses his tormentors and plunges out into the Ashet night. It works brilliantly. Again and again in his plays he stirred the sleeping dragons of his unconscious and, as Tyrone Guthrie said, provided his audiences with moments of commanding brilliance, worthy of being judged by the very highest standards. At the end of the day, or the end of the play, however, he did have a difficulty in resolving his dramas. Too often he either opted for domesticity and a cup of tea or left his Last Judgements to God, failing to pursue his vision to its, perhaps alarming, conclusion.

I do not think, as was alleged, that this was a technical fault. He knew plenty about technique. I think it came from a real moral dilemma. The sort of person he was, and the experiences which he had had, made him distrustful of the Dionysiac side of his nature. The influence of the admirable Dr Mavor may not always have been good for Mr Bridie. Meanwhile, he was learning his trade at the feet of Ayliff, a master if ever there was one.

A few brief examples give the tone of the correspondence between the apprentice playwright and the very experienced director. It appears that Bridie had been anxious that the part of Lady Katharine in the final act of *A Sleeping Clergyman* should be played with authenticity and had recommended Miss Pamela Carme (later married to Henry Sherek, the impresario) who was, I think, the daughter of a Duke. Ayliff replied:

> Rest. Calme yourself perturbed spirit for she of that ilk has been definitely engaged. We have put the plebean SPOTLIGHT into the wastepaper basket and are now casting from Debrett. Ernest Thesiger will probably be Marshall and Sir Basil Bartlett (second Bart?), Purley. Phyllis Shand who will appear as the prostitute is a personal friend of the Duke of Richmond & Gordon (or some such personage) and has actually dined with His Grace, her eye on the bell the while in case of eventualities which did not occur. Would you like Violet, Duchess of Rutland, for Mrs Hannah?
>
> And don't get cold feet and talk rot about the play which you may have written but obviously can't appreciate. It'll be put over by hook or by crook and I've no doubt, if I'm spared, I'll be guided which nefarious process to choose.

And when the play was about to transfer to the Piccadilly Theatre:

> Miss Fordred, you may be interested to know, is not entirely satisfied with her costumes. She tells me that she shudders to think what Miss Martita Hunt would say if she were asked to wear such inferior garments. In the end she shuddered to hear what I had to say about Miss Martita Hunt.

It was not long before Bridie himself felt the edge of Ayliff's tongue. Robert Donat, a close friend with whom he was to have

82

many disagreements over the years, was a martyr to asthma and Ayliff's careful guardianship of his star was disturbed when the author ventured some comments on his performance. Ayliff wrote:

> Beloved Physician, Donat has just been to see me in a state of complete and utter hopelessness as the result of a letter from you. If you want to write to him please write about his health which is far from satisfactory, and let me deal with any weaknesses that may crop up in his performance. As a producer you are a quack and, with the best intentions, are a potential nuisance to actors. Why on earth didn't you write to me? I know how to talk to actors without sending them into the depth of despair or swelling their heads to bursting point. Also I know how small is the difference between a top-notch performance and one that doesn't get there. Donat's nerves are all to bits and in a small flat with a monthly nurse of complete efficiency his life is, naturally, unendurable — he hasn't slept for weeks — so to mend matters you write and lead him to believe that he is ruining your play and ought never to have gone on the stage at all! It has taken me the whole morning putting things right. He's going to sleep at a friend's house out at Hampstead so that he'll have quiet and fresh air after the shows. I've also discussed his performance with him and pointed out the danger points. I saw the show through at the matinée on Saturday and found nothing to complain of beyond a tiny soft spot which was accidental and not likely to happen again.
>
> Please, please, please, when next you have cold feet write to me and I will interpret your complainings without creating a stampede.

Visiting Physicians in our hospitals are not accustomed to being talked to in this fashion. Rather they have a Nursing Sister, a number of Assistants, a Resident, and a bunch of young nurses who hang on their every word. Dr Mavor, however, took no offence. And Mr Bridie was eager to learn. But, family illnesses apart, it must have been a stressful time. And the stresses were not purely intellectual.

In 1934 Tyrone Guthrie was directing a play which Bridie had written for Flora Robson in which she, who had complained to him that she seemed fated to play 'frustrated spinsters with an evil mind', blossomed as the female pirate, Mary Read. The play was an extravaganza and Flora played opposite Robert Donat (in a

Robert Donat as Edward Earle, and Flora Robson in the title-role of
Mary Read, 1934. Photograph by Tunbridge.

rather thankless part). Another actress in the play, however, had
developed some kind of close relationship with the author. A friend
of hers once remarked to me that, 'X was mad to think Osborne
would leave Rona for her', which, at the least, suggests that she did.

Careful reading between the lines of various letters, and
what Rona herself told me, establishes that a Sunday morning
assignation in London was discovered when the lady in question
sent an enthusiastic confirmatory telegram to my father's Club — the
Glasgow Art Club. As it arrived after he had left for the London train,
the Manager phoned Rona and, on request, read the telegram to her.

Rona, on hearing the telegram, decamped — I've no idea why
— to Aberdeen of all places and took some days or weeks to be
begged back. Once returned, as I've said, I think she made very
sure that such an incident would not be repeated, deploying her
virtuoso repertoire of psychosomatic illnesses to the purpose as
required. I don't think she was given cause to be anxious.

Osborne had been staying with the Guthries and Tony had, it
seems, written sympathetically about the situation. Osborne replied:

My Dear Tony,

Your perception of what is touching and heart-rending and ridiculous, all at the same time, in people and things is such that a person would like to tell you all about it as he would to God — except for this, that we can't help feeling that God doesn't quite understand what a person is after and how it upsets a person. With you, on the other hand . . .

I think you know that I have done the damnedest for M.R. [Mary Read] that could be done by one whose sense of the incongruous (a sense on which he is accustomed to rely) had been battered out of gear. Honest, chum, I did. But pray that when you are 46 and into smooth water you will be either good, bad or middling and not blown about by the Devil or the Almighty into a whirlwind of noble renunciations and gestures and heartbreaks and idiocies and anger and pain and delirium and irrelevancies and absurdities and cruelties and longings; these things are tolerable and salutary in the young, but bad for the blood pressure in the stout and middle-aged and the very blazes for their friends, relatives and lovers. So much for that. I'll tell you some day the bits you haven't divined. The circumstances may not be unusual, but they have their unusual angles. And so much for that. Don't be afraid that I'll relapse into self-pity or self-contempt. I've a Scotch conceit of myself that blames misfortune upon Providence and a Scotch theology that teaches me that I have no influence on that remarkable phenomenon.

And I am really less selfish and self-centred than my neighbours, though you could never tell it from this bloody letter. So much for that. I mean really. Talk about it to me any time you want to or would like to help a person who has gone a bit lame, but don't write about it; for your letters are received in this house with general rapture, a rapture that would be clouded if the PAST were invoked. Do this, though. Give X a shove on when and where and how you can. I can't and I think she's an artist who just waits the right métier to burst into flame. . . .

Early in 1935 Dr Mavor was given his own wards at the Victoria Infirmary, becoming, as we said, a Chief, and wrote to a friend that he would have to spend less time writing plays. He didn't.

He wrote, that year, *Storm in a Teacup*, *The King of Nowhere* and *The Black Eye*. In January he worked on his first film script, for Berthold Viertel, and met the German playwright Bruno Frank:

> This was my first film script, and I helped Viertel and Bruno Frank to make it. We made it in three weeks. At the end of that time Viertel stood up, raised his eyes to heaven and said, 'We haf composed the first film masterpiece. I shall be able to shoot this film vord for vord with the same reverence as I would give to directing a play of Shakespeare on stage. And now you will stay for a little and explain it to Micky Balcon.'
>
> I did not wait to see Mr Balcon, but it was reported to me that he summed up the script with the one word 'Lousy'. I do not know whether this is correct, but I heard no more of the script. Our efforts were not, however, entirely of noneffect. Viertel said to Frank that it was a great pity his comedy *Sturm im Wasserglas* [*Storm in a Teacup*] was impossible to adapt into the English idiom. A fortnight later I had done an adaptation. A week later my agent sold it to the Haymarket Theatre.

In the event, the Haymarket's option on *Storm in a Teacup* lapsed after six months, but it was finally produced, directed by W. G. Fay, on February 5th 1936, the night of the death of King George V. In time it did get to the Haymarket where it ran for a year, and the new King had a command performance of part of it in Lady Cunard's drawing-room, the Court being still in mourning. There's grandeur for you. In the meantime Bridie had written *The Black Eye* in which the remarkable young actor Stephen Haggard had a notable success under the management of C. B. Cochran.

On the strength of all this the Mavors bought a rather grand Scottish baronial house just outside the agreeable village of Drymen, some seventeen miles north of Glasgow, to which we all moved in October 1936.

II

Glasgow, whose urban delights are, perhaps, revealed only to born and bred Glaswegians, is blessed with magnificent surroundings. Driving to Drymen one arrives suddenly on the crest of a north-facing hill at the Stockiemuir. On one's left is a remarkable rock-cleft called the Whangie, which, it is believed, was created when the Devil struck the rock-face with his tail, knocking it over into the Clyde where it is known as Ailsa Craig. *En face*, to the north, is Loch Lomond, dominated by its Ben, and the hills of Argyll and Stirlingshire.

Gateside, the new house, was a red sandstone pile standing on a bluff east of the village of Drymen and facing towards Killearn (where Rona's mother and sister lived happily for thirty years) and the Campsie Fells with their striking outcrop, Dumgoyne. The Mavors were given to inventing derogatory names for their many houses — Rockbank, at Craigendoran, was later christened 'Sewage View' by Rona. Osborne called Gateside 'Tinned Salmon Castle', but it had a good deal of charm. When acquired it had a spire, later demolished, over the entrance tower and a beautiful old fly-wheeled engine which pumped electricity into a score of wet batteries. It had also a walled garden with two vines, red and white — an army of rats uniquely passed in the night and demolished the crop that first year — and, also under glass, two beautiful camellias. These were looked after by Mr Rhind, the gardener.

There was also a short series of chauffeurs-cum-odd-job-men who were less successful until Jimmy Vickers came along. At least three of his family were to work for the Mavors, and he later became a local councillor and was, from the beginning, a cheerful and supportive chap in a house beset by a good deal of troubles, falling trees, drying

Ian Dalrymple and O. H. Mavor working on the film adaptation of *Storm in a Teacup*, 1936.

pumps, broken fences, dry rot, bats and, I think, though I'm not sure, death-watch beetles. Country life, then as now, balanced its bucolic pleasures with endless responsibilities. For the first year at Gateside, Dr Mavor was driven every morning in the Wolseley to his wards at the Victoria Infirmary. The other member of the staff was Lindsay Galloway, later a well-known writer for television, who brought his wife to a cottage in the village and handled the correspondence and took dictation, direct to the typewriter. He was to return at a later stage and my father's irregular but intensive hours of work, and disinclinations for work, seemed to suit, too, with Lindsay's personality.

Rona was very fond of Gateside and enjoyed being chatelaine. She won a fierce loyalty from those who worked for her, I think because she knew what she wanted and never hesitated to say so if she failed to achieve it. The house was always filled with flowers and she was an excellent hostess. Mrs Hutcheson, the cook, had come from 6 Woodlands Terrace and the new Aga cooker, after initial problems, produced Lucullan dinners. There were several guest bedrooms and lots of bathrooms. We played rough cricket on the lawns and my father even attempted a turf cricket pitch in the middle of a field of extremely tuffety grass. He borrowed a shotgun from his brother Jack, but shot only the occasional rabbit — as did Robert and I with a .22. I recollect demolishing a tiny rabbit with about seven airgun bullets. It happened to be the day of George VI's coronation and Osborne remarked that the rabbit had not, alas, been a good subject of the new King for very long. Some cows grazed over the hedge. Apart from the Wolseley — later a Rover — Rona had a splendid old Austin with about twenty removable cellophane windows and a collapsible hood.

The main project, as the Mavors moved into Gateside, was the film of *Storm in a Teacup*. Ian Dalrymple, who was to write the screen-play for the film (with Rex Harrison and Vivien Leigh) wrote to me:

> In 1936 Victor Saville set up as an independent Producer to make films at Alexander Korda's new large studios at Denham. I had edited or supervised the editing of many of the Films which he had produced for the Gainsborough and Gaumont-British companies, and now he took me on as his script-writer. He had bought the film rights of STORM IN A TEACUP and my second job for Victor was to adapt the play for the screen. While other writers seemed always to retire to Mediterranean resorts or other European beauty-spots, to my chagrin I was despatched to Glasgow to work. The next fortnight turned out to be the best of my life to that date: for the man with whom I was to collaborate was 'James Bridie', and his and Rona's kindness and hospitality led to a lasting friendship.

In November 1936 Bridie wrote to him from Gateside:

> The electric light is on (though the fittings aren't up) and we hope to have the new pump and a steady supply of water next week.
>
> In the meantime I am surrounded by idle hands open to clutch my hard-earned savings. I shall go bankrupt, I think, in April next.
>
> I am sweating my soul out to finish a play. I'll then get on with Susannah, Benvenuto Cellini, a thriller, a sentimental Scots play about Auld Robin Gray, an Esther play & a really good David play with possibly one about the Blessingtons and a moral domestic comedy. This will take me to Christmas.

D

Rex Harrison as Frank Burdon and Vivien Leigh as Victoria in the film version of *Storm in a Teacup*.

And on February 14th 1937:

> We are a bit in the doldrums here. Young Robert took an osteomyelitis of his right shin bone about six weeks ago and, according to modern methods of treatment, has to lie about with his leg in plaster with all manner of revolting end-products of destruction seeping through it and making the house stink like a ruined cellar at Ypres. . . .
>
> Rona is only fairly well and I have run into slack water with the plays. The two I have finished don't seem, for the moment, to be saleable.
>
> I think I have reached the stage attained by Shaw, Maugham and many lesser men. When they really know their job and how to hold and entertain an audience, the London managers (whom God preserve) will have none of them.
>
> And, by the way, I was cheering myself by reading my own earlier works and marvelling at what a genius I had then. . . .

Sylvia Coleridge as Nurse Appleby and Laurence Olivier as Vivaldi in *The King of Nowhere*. Photograph by Debenham. Reproduced from the *Sketch*, 23 March 1938.

This was, indeed, one of the longest pauses between plays in Bridie's career. After *Storm in a Teacup*, which opened in February 1936, there was no new play until *Susannah and the Elders* was given a Sunday night performance by a Club theatre in October 1937, being followed by *The King of Nowhere* with Olivier, at the Old Vic, in March 1938. In January 1938 he resigned from the Victoria Infirmary.

Maybe it isn't good for playwrights — perhaps especially Scottish Calvinist playwrights — to move to comfortable country seats (or, nowadays, swimming pools in California). Artists, of course, must

'Mr Guthrie regarding Mr J. Bridie with doglike devotion.' One of a series of caricatures of Tyrone Guthrie by Mavor.

move on. They cannot stay, literally or metaphorically, in the same place, and success, too, has its problems. When *The King of Nowhere* was performed, after many false starts, it was Bridie's sixteenth play to be professionally performed since *The Switchback* ten years before. He had crossed the Rubicon and burnt his boats, but he felt that he was still being treated by the London managers as 'Miss Menopause of Bournemouth'.

At first he took out his angst on Donat, whom he could not persuade to play Vivaldi, the paranoid actor who becomes, briefly, a Dictator, in *The King of Nowhere*. And then on Tony Guthrie who was, in Mr Bridie's view, wasting his time and talent on commercial successes, like Dodie Smith's *Sweet Aloes*, rather than the plays of Shakespeare or James Bridie. I think an exchange of letters about *Susannah and the Elders*, demonstrates both the relationship of the two, very witty and devoted men, and something of the crisis in the author who, I suspect, was projecting his own problems on to Guthrie and the theatre of the time.

Guthrie had written on July 15th 1937:

Well I've read *Susannah* and I think it is very good: nearly all the time very amusing, and wise and endearing and original, and at its best (which I think the after-dinner scene; and the things that are between and above the lines in the scenes between the two old men) is A.1., $^{10}/_{10}$ and gets a red rosette.

And yet — now please remember that it is more friendly of me to try and say truthfully what I think and feel, than just to bolster you up with pleasant things and feed your wicked sinful timidity — if I were Binkie B or Bronnie A [Hugh Beaumont of H. M. Tennents and Bronson Albery] i.e. if I were a 'commercial' manager and depended on the production of a trading commodity in dramatic form to pay the high rate of interest on loaned money demanded by my Jewish backers (Mr B) or my rapacious old Aunt Minnie (Mr A) I wouldn't consider it for a moment. And I think the screamy-outy tone of your last letter most unjustified. [A proposed revival of *Tobias and the Angel* had fallen through and Bridie blamed Guthrie, casting a few aspersions also on Mr Albery's approach to theatre management.] Why the hell should these people do your plays? They're not in the business to do good plays — they want to make money and to please the sort of people who'll buy stalls and make them knights [which only Mr Albery achieved] and have them out to supper and things. Besides, most of your plays aren't even good plays — they have streaks of most dazzling and commanding brilliance but they're weak at the knees — e.g. the last act of the Anatomist; of the Switchback; of the King of Nowhere; one is beguiled by the brilliant bits into judging you by the highest standards and with real reverence — and then you tire suddenly of your subject (like a cat tires suddenly of playing or washing — you are *very* like a cat) and walk off with your furry tail waving, with pretty little delicate steps.

To return to *Susannah*: like Binkie, I don't think I quite understand it either. Is it just an anecdote (beautifully retailed) with a precept that we must not be unkind in our judgement of 'horrid old men', because there's so much good in the worst of us etc.? I don't mean that that isn't enough. It's a little sermon that, preached by you at your best, would easily keep me intent for 2½ hours in a theatre. But there seemed to be a further theme less explicit — but I don't know what it is. What was Daniel? What did he mean at the end? I'd like to have read it again but Spencer [Curtis Brown] was insistent that the script must go at once to Dr Czinner [husband of Elizabeth Bergner]. . .

I hope to goodness Miss Bergner isn't to 'bring it to life'; turning Susannah into her own patented brand of canned elf. . . .

Sweet Aloes was on an altogether inferior plane in mentality. But in its low grade it was an immensely competent piece of *professional painstaking craftsmanship*. And as such had something about it that I don't think any of your plays has fully realized. And while I don't pretend that your worst play is not immeasurably better than *Sweet Aloes*; I think it is mean-spirited in you to grudge its success with the Binkies. . . .

Now you can go ahead and write a *filthy* letter in reply.

Bridie was quick to reply, on July 19th:

I wrote you eight pages of dignified invective and showed it to Rona. Rona said that, while no doubt it was all quite true, if she were Judy she would be very angry. I do not want Judy to be even mildly annoyed at me so I am not sending that letter, though I am certain you would have enjoyed it.

The gist of it was that your 'Business is Business' attitude sits very ill upon you and has led you into a wicked blunder. The handwriting is the handwriting of T. Guthrie but the sentiments are those of a Manager's Nark. . . .

My whole complaint against the London Theatre can be comprised in that curious vulgarity of outlook that makes even you quite casually and carelessly put down your dissatisfaction with the last acts of The Anatomist and The Switchback to swindling gimcrack work by the author. If the charge were true, I would have no right to your friendship or to any consideration at all. But it is not true. These last acts were written carefully and passionately and they contain an expression of what happened to be my philosophy of life at the time. Your attitude to them is exactly that of the Art Critic of the Tailor and Cutter (who likes his buttons right) and of Constant Reader of Peg's Paper (who likes a story rounded and finished — preferably with a good rousing lie). I am so much entitled to finish my composition as it seems to me *right* as Sickert is to finish his compositions as it seems to him right — that is, if I've earned any status at all as an artist. This does not in the least cut out the possibility of criticism. Obviously these two plays show signs of rawness and inexperience. But it is *not* criticism to ask me to paint pictures like those nice, shiny portraits in the Academy. . . .

Good craftsmanship can be displayed on light and trivial objects and I think I can appreciate Noel Coward and Dodie Smith as well as my neighbours. In N.C.'s case good craftsmanship goes right up into the genius class; but Dodie is her own justification. But, if you weren't pixillated you'd see that a set of tame theatrical tricks are not craftsmanship at all. Any smart boy can learn them. Any evil-minded schoolgirl has them naturally at her finger-ends. I know them all myself, by this time.

You know all this as well as I do and that's why I make a solemn appeal to you to get back to your own values and judgement and stop degrading yourself — for that is what you are really doing. You have a perfect right to play with the dirty little boys and girls in the back court if it amuses you. But don't sit down and write me *their* opinions as if they mattered a damn or were other than the opinions of dirty little boys and girls.

I wish I had sent you the other letter, because this is terribly like John Hilton on the wireless. Do come up here and talk to me — if only for a week-end.

Both friendships, of course, survived. Guthrie, and Donat, wrote explaining the parameters of the London stage and Mr Bridie, quite properly, continued to complain that artists should serve their art and not the 'very inferior business men who cater so badly for the public'.

His own art, however, was not going well. For all the idyllic pleasures of Gateside and the comforts of Rona's well-run household, the plays of this period nearly all seemed, at some point, to come unstuck. *The King of Nowhere* began as an extravaganza about a paranoid actor who escapes from an asylum and is persuaded by a frustrated spinster of great wealth to become leader of a Scottish Fascist Party. Much pressure was put upon Donat to play the part but he, I think rightly, resisted it. In the end Olivier played it, though *not* directed by Guthrie. The play wasn't a success. What had started as a play about the actor, became, as three years passed with the rise of dictatorship in Europe, a play about dictators. Guthrie was right when he wrote, shortly after the play opened, that 'the dictator stuff is a red herring', and, in 1938, plays about dictators in which the fact of dictatorship was a red herring were unlikely to catch the public mood.

Guthrie's letter, in his most brilliant and witty style, continues:

> The relationship between the shallow brilliant man and the decent noble frustrated woman says something that applies to everybody — both in regard to their relations with other people and their battles with themselves. . . .
>
> I can't see that you've said anything interesting at all about dictators. And it is unfortunate that the play should be produced at a moment when public consciousness is concentrated on politics . . . because I think the political psychologising is much the shallowest and most second-hand in the play. . . .
>
> I think the play *is* untidy — I agree absolutely with Ivor Brown — and the untidiness of your work is detrimental to one's appreciation of it . . . the meaning is hard to find because the actual structure never seems to be part of the meaning. Your plays are like jerry-built cathedrals covered with imaginative and exquisitely made ornaments. One is deterred from going in to worship partly because one suspects that the whole affair may come crashing down; but principally because the door is designed for exit only and one has to force an entrance through the roof.

Whether or not the criticism was just, it was clever criticism. I don't, myself, agree that audiences had difficulty knowing, in a Bridie play, where they were or what was going on, and I think Bridie would have denied any desire to build cathedrals or to invite people in to worship. But he *was* having problems with his dramaturgy. None of his next four plays, produced in 1938 and 1939, made much impact. *Susannah and the Elders*, another biblical adaptation, achieved only a Sunday night production and never made the West End.

Susannah, one of the author's favourite plays, is, like *Tobias and the Angel*, a more-or-less straight transcription from the Apocrypha. There is, however, something wrong with it. The crime of Susannah's seduction by the wicked old Elders is splendidly told but, at the end, Daniel, who has solved the case and struck a blow for the exiled Israelites, has doubts — for which the audience is given no reason — whether, indeed, he has 'spoken on God's behalf'. And the Reader cautions: 'The old story says that these Judges who did this wickedness were false and evil to the bone; but who knows the heart of a man and what moves in that darkness?'

What is wrong with it is that the story, what Aristotle called the *praxis*, which is straightforward (a crime is committed, a detective questions the suspects and exposes the crime) proves not to be what-the-play-is-about.

Aristotle believed, rightly, that the action (*praxis*) of the play should precisely enshrine what the play *says*. There are notable examples of plays which ignore this doctrine; for example, Ibsen's *Brand*, where the whole life of the hero — a passionate minister of religion who sacrifices everything, his wife and child included, to his vision — is questioned when, from the snow avalanche which destroys him, there comes a voice saying, 'He is the God of Love'.

Again, there is a dislocation between the *mores* of Dr Mavor, and much of the world, and the imagination of Mr Bridie. Daniel can forgive the old rogues their love for Susannah at the end, although the play has demonstrated their guilt and granted him a triumph not only for himself but for his Israelite people.

Lancelot, too, which was first written in 1939, proved recalcitrant. Its later history is recounted in Chapter Thirteen. Again, I believe, he picked up, and marvellously retold, an old story, but had a problem with the *praxis* which simply didn't reflect what he wanted to say. It is notable that these two plays are in a new, somewhat distanced, somewhat bejewelled style. They have an elegant, polished surface, like a Persian tile.

The relationship between an author and his plays varies from age to age and country to country. In North America, as has been observed, the writer is expected to bleed over the keyboard of his

Mrs Rona Mavor with her sons Robert and Ronald. Photograph by
T. & R. Annan, Glasgow.

typewriter. This was not the way of Shakespeare or Congreve or
Racine. It is possible that Bridie was beginning to develop a style
which might have led to a new classicism: but events caught up

with him. He was not prepared to retire to a cork-lined room, like Proust, when the world was entering a new crisis.

What happened to *The King of Nowhere* was significant. The world, and its horrors, was looming too dark on the horizon for a dramatist who wanted to forgive the world not condemn it. Eric Linklater records a conversation with my father about Mihailovic, the Yugoslav partisan leader, in which Bridie remarked that there was much meat for tragedy in our times but added that he would only write comedy, as tragedy would involve insulting the human race.

In such times he had no doubt about where he ought to be, and what he ought to be about. He was no Cassandra. The one play, modestly presented at the Perth Theatre as part of their new theatre Festival (another casualty of the Second World War) which shines from this rather sticky period is *The Golden Legend of Shults*. This was a lively piece of Scotch picaresque in which the experienced James Gibson was marvellous as the decent little Glasgow burglar, Davie Cooper. Finding the world 'outside' corrupt and unsavoury, Davie buys and bulldozes the ghastly seaside town of Shults and, before leaving for the South Seas with Annie, the maid from the hotel, reaches a fine, and quite unpolished, eloquence:

> Whatameantosay, I'd kind of like you to . . . Listen, chums, try to do better by yourselfs. Honest, chums, take a look at yourselfs. Shults is an awful-like place. It's not life, what you're doing, humdrum cheating and boozing and chewing the rag and scaring off the Devil in the kirk on the Sabbath. Honest, chums, you'd be better off if you was sauvages. . . .
>
> Whatameantosay, there's some made one way and some another, and if those that's made one way would only let those that's made the other way alone, because how does anybody know what's going on inside a block's heid?

John Grierson was to say that Bridie, as no Scotsman since Burns, had the greatest native virtue of his race, 'knowing when to throw the rhetoric over your shoulder and come down to the good earth'.

Be that as it may, shortly, very shortly, after the première of *What Say They?* at the Malvern Festival, Mr Bridie had reverted to an earlier persona. He became, at the age of fifty-one, Lieutenant Mavor in the Royal Army Medical Corps for the second time in his life.

12

In the autumn of 1939 Robert and I went to Merchiston Castle School in Edinburgh. It wasn't an institution of which my father entirely approved:

> There are, indeed, some advantages to be gained from attendance at a good public school. A boy gains physical toughness, pleasant manners, confidence, a communal and even a public spirit, self-respect, a kind of loyalty, a tolerance of discipline, a fair general education, some independence of mind, a certain magnanimity and a powerful social and economic advantage, at least in England. The last gain is unfair. He owes it to a particular way of speaking and to the sentimentality of old public schoolboys in key positions.

But it helped to clear the decks.

He wrote, on September 27th, to Ian Dalrymple:

> We have moved (having sold our house in Drymen) into Glasgow, to a noble and beautiful terrace house full of filth, with a gold ceiling on the drawing room and eight feet of water in the cellar; and three faulty lighting systems one on top of the other and all condemned by the City Electrician. We have had workmen in it for three months whose wages we shall have to pay and we are camping out with an ex-cook of ours who is suffering from erythema multiforme and her husband who is a taxi-driver and subject to moods of depression. . . .
>
> I have been passed for foreign service in the RAMC. I made direct for the tortoise's armpit or I should have gone mad. . . . Rona has got a sort of semi-offer to go as house-keeper to a posh

hospital in Perthshire or Stirlingshire or somewhere, but I don't know whether she'll take it. I feel wicked for deserting her to loaf about in an Officers' Mess — but that is better than going into an asylum, because she will get family pay and a pension when I come home with shell shock after a few weeks. . . .

This was, of course, just fun. But one cannot but be sorry for Rona, so lightly dismissed to a totally unsuitable and, as it proved, unavailable war task. If, and it is at the least arguable, Lieutenant Mavor's return to the colours was also a flight from Mr Bridie's problems he, unlike O'Neill, was far from abandoning his wife and family. He was to write to Rona almost daily, as he had written to his mother in the previous war. These letters — over 251 of them — deserve a book to themselves. They are quite as interesting for what they leave out as for what they contain. They are affectionate. They are full of marvellous descriptions and observations of the, rather ordinary, people he met and the daily life on a Hospital Ship and a Military Hospital in Belfast. They are almost innocent of literary matters. They contain some fascinating sketches of philosophy but on that topic, and on the politics of the time, they are not profound. They are full of — I fear somewhat half-hearted — hopes that he will get leave or that Rona may visit him, that he may be transferred to some more overtly useful work. But through them shines a real delight in being back in a simpler and less-demanding world of men and medicine and day-to-day duties and pleasures.

He wrote many times of his ability to hibernate or rather — and I think Bagheera in Kipling's Mowgli stories is the model — to climb a tree like a panther and sleep until fierce activity is again required of him.

Before leaving for the wars he had dictated, very fast, his autobiography, *One Way of Living*, to Lindsay Galloway. In it he wrote:

> I find myself at fifty in a pleasant and even enviable material position. I live in a comfortable house in agreeable surroundings. I have a wife and family of whom I am fond and who are fond of me. I have an overdraft at the Bank, but my Bank Agent still smiles when I speak to him and I am able to afford many minor luxuries. I belong to some good clubs and have reached a respectable position in at least two difficult professions. I am under the orders of nobody except

the tax-gatherers and the police. I have several friends and no enemies except one lady who writes me anonymous postcards. I sleep well. I have no troublesome illnesses. I have ten times as much leisure as anybody between the ranks of a millionaire and a tramp.

If I suggest that this was, perhaps, just great for Dr Mavor but not enough for Mr Bridie it is because I am trying to trace what he, himself, called 'the Sinbadism of the Soul'. In doing so I become ever more conscious that many, even most, people who knew him will disagree with me, and that I may be wrong. Walter Elliot, who knew him better than anyone, was to say, in a memorial programme on the B.B.C.:

> One of the things [about him] was that he came into existence full-blown. I have known him all his life — I was at school with him and at university with him and at camp with him and elsewhere. He was full-blown when he originated. I remember him almost exactly the same when he was a schoolboy. . . .
>
> I think that he had an extraordinary power of existing inside of himself. I think that one of the things that we always were anxious to do was to attract his attention, really, because we felt that if we attracted his attention we ourselves had done something worthwhile. . . .
>
> One would make a mistake if one thought that Osborne had ever done anything unintentionally. . . . But the fact of the matter was that he was an awfully considerate man. . . . But, mind you, he had a certain pitiless quality which we should not lose sight of. I think it shows most strongly in that play of his about the Trojan War, The Queen's Comedy. That pitiless nature, you know, is a quality of the Scottish nation. We are not merciless, but it is a pitiless nation; and where he derived it particularly from, I think, was that he was an engineer. After all, he was himself a doctor but he was the son of a great engineer, and the brother of a great engineer. That quality of precision, that unrelenting quality, which is the essence of the engineer, was very much part of his make-up. But of course what we are trying to describe is a genius. He was an authentic genius and it was the same at the beginning of his life as at the end.

The rather elderly Lieutenant Mavor was posted to the Royal Victoria Hospital at Netley, and then joined the *Atlantis*, which hung around Falmouth and then made trips to Alexandria and the north-west coast of Norway to evacuate wounded. On the latter trip she was, briefly, chased by the *Scharnhorst*. His letters to Rona are, above all, considerate, if not always frank.

1st December, 1939

Here I am in this peculiar place. It has taken until now (5.30) to find any kind of bearings, & I don't yet know who, what or where I am. . . .

2nd December, 1939

The sun shines bright. I have been given a job — quite a pleasing one. I am in charge of No. 8 Hospital Ship Unit, no other MO's having turned up yet, so it is my first command in this War. I have spent the morning quite happily in *my* Orderly Room & in the fresh air watching *my* young militiamen learning squad drill. My Orderly Room is a bench in a stable with one other ship and half a dozen ambulance trains. I have a couple of really good sergeants, one bad and one good corporal, & 60 odd men. . . . It seems likely that we shall be here for a good long time. The troops have to be trained, sent out for trial trips, returned again & so on before we are fit to sail as a unit. It is rather a different story from Tweseldown in 1914. We have regular N.C.O.'s & the troops are in most pansified huts with iron bedsteads, spring mattresses & lockers for themselves. They also have baths, real W.C.'s & all the modern conveniences, though I foresee a certain amount of mud. . . .

6th December, 1939

I got your Monday's letter today & it pleased me. A darned good letter, if you don't mind my saying so! It came at a good time, because I had a good night's sleep after a shivery day & a half [inoculations] &, apart from a sore arm, feel none too bad today. This little time has showed me how I have grown into a pampered pup. You do everything for me & make me contented & intolerable. It wanted a slight temperature hanging over a miserable fire in a horrid little fireplace with a plush hanging (brown plush hangings) on the mantelpiece; a wet and windy mile to walk for my meals & the same (blacked out) back to a bumpy bed in a draughty bedroom; and no bathroom; to make me realise that, besides being a knock-down charmer, Mrs R. B. Mavor has the gift of making a person comfortable. I forgot to mention the Mess — Oh, my God! It is a frigid mausoleum with fires surrounded by fat Majors & giving out no heat anyway. There are two or three pleasant enough men but nobody quite in my line of gaiety and conversation. And, I am happy to say, the Great Mister Bridie means nothing to them. So you will see that all this is excellent for my Soul. Loafing in the fresh air is also not bad for my body, so there are prospects of Salvation through endurance — two faculties I find, to my delight, that I have not yet lost.

15th December, 1939

I am back in the billet. It is DAMNED cold, but they have lit a fire and it is blinking up & life will soon be bearable. Since I wrote last, four or five hours ago, I have been enjoying life in a quiet way. After I posted your letter I went back to the Registrar's Office & sat down at the big desk with my back to the fire & read the Orders by Lieut.-General Bertie Thingummybob & also King's Regulations which are full of quiet amusement for the judicious. At intervals I answered the telephone and signed railway warrants & what not. At about four, two lads came in & fixed up the blackout boards on the window. Shortly after the O.C. Hospital drifted in & began to talk to me while I waded through a big bunch of things to sign. At that moment the telephone bell rang & I dealt very expertly with a deaf old Colonel of the Royal Artillery & then the lights fused & we were left in darkness. So we took the board off the window & I finished signing my chits on the window sill. The Colonel then invited me to tea to meet his Mem-Sahib. So I went.

One should never judge a man until one has seen his wife. The Mem-Sahib was trained at the R.A.D.A. in 1915 and then gave it up to 'go into the Army'. She'd be pretty good as one of the witches in Macbeth. She goes round the London theatres with a comrade of the R.A.D.A. who is an unsuccessful actress & pulls it to bits because, knowing something about it, she is very critical, bless her heart. . . . I showed off like blazes. The dear Colonel had never heard such brilliance. He is really a very nice man.

24th January, 1940

We had a most delightful Burns Night. . . . Eight of us sat down to dinner at the Dirty Duck and the dinner consisted of soup, haggis and whisky. MacHardy, MacCallum & I then read Burns aloud till the restaurant was invaded by a young Royal Naval Air Service man and his fiancée. They sat down by the fire & embarrassed us very much — by their presence, simply. However, it turned out that he was a Scotsman called Coates. So I proposed the health and happiness of him and his fiancée instead of the Immortal Memory, & a decorous & pleasant evening was had by all. The fiancée was very beautiful but very dumb & sat & beamed at us all over a glass of sherry. Brown came in then and made an admirable speech in German on the character of Hitler. We sang 'Deutschland Über Alles' & the meeting adjourned.

25th February, 1940

Last night I sat for a bit [this was off Alexandria] and talked to Agnew, Robinson and the two Wireless Operators about Peru and Petros and Brazil and Jerusalem, Madagascar, North and South Amerikee, to say nothing of Wishaw, which is the home of Sparks No. 1. Tiring of this, I went off to bed about ten, only to be disturbed by the noise of running feet. . . . I was rewarded for going to the gangway by meeting the Sergeant Major, returning, slightly lit up, from seeing the sights. He was carrying a large bouquet of flowers. He said, 'Look, Sir. My flowers. Are they not beautiful?' I said, 'Yes, Sergeant Major, but I am told that they die very quickly in this country.' He said, 'Ah, no. Look at those anemones. They will last forever!' I said, 'I bet you sixpence they will be dead by tomorrow morning.' He said, 'What? Only sixpence, Sir? Oh, Sir, I have been to see *The Hunchback of Notre Dame*. It is truly magnificent.' I said, 'Is Mr Laughton better than Lon Chaney?' He said, 'Infinitely, Sir, infinitely. I cried my eyes out. The tears were running down my cheeks.' . . . This peculiar conversation so amused me that I went upstairs to tell it to the others and did not get to bed until twelve. The Chief Engineer came up from his oil tanks and we stood on deck awhile spitting into the ditch. He said to me, 'I have been sizing up the Doctors here. You seem to me to be much the best man among the lot o' them.' I said, 'Naturally. I am a bloody genius.'

5th July, 1940

Dinner with the Robbies last night at the Red Lion on their arrival back from their honeymoon. Mrs R. is a nice, pretty, pleasant but silly little thing, I think. I had to work fairly hard to make the evening go. My big success was when that dour waiter with the bulldog face was asked by Robbie if they had a double room empty. The waiter asked him to repeat it and then said, 'I see!' very loudly and with a most peculiar expression. He then ran away. To Ann's terror, I sent for him and asked him what he meant by 'I see!'. He was filled with confusion and said that he had said 'I'll go and see'. He later stopped Robbie and gave him a much more elaborate and quite different excuse. We were very merry over it, having little enough to amuse us.

And one could go on. . . .

The letters cease about this time, as the *Atlantis* was posted to the Holy Loch, down the River Clyde. They continue in April 1941 when Major Mavor was put in charge of a psychiatric hospital at Purdysburn, just outside Belfast. During his first months in Northern Ireland we all, Robert and I on school holidays, moved to Belfast and were there for 'the Belfast Blitz' — I'm sure there was more than one — which I enjoyed, as an aesthetic spectacle, from an upstairs window, all fires and fireworks. In April, however, Rona returned to Glasgow and the letters continued, becoming, I think, franker and more useful. It is a shame that Rona destroyed *her* side of the correspondence, which Osborne kept. She was a good, spontaneous letter writer, which he never was. But I think the war period, interrupted by leaves and visits, worked well for their relationship. The Belfast letters — and he had more stimulating company among his colleagues, and a livelier social life in the city — contain more protein than those from the ship.

The wireless was disturbing this morning about Glasgow. I do hope it wasn't so bad as it sounded. I was glad to think you were out of it. Ours, last night, was 'only a little one' and I slept through it as they didn't think it worth while wakening me.

The tough old girl who brings her beauty chorus out to do basket-making with the patients turned up yesterday, complete with helmet and flannel breeks and son. Her house had been blown down and she didn't think she could collect the beauty chorus in time for this week. She had spent the night trotting about among dropping bombs and digging people out and was a little dirty but as fresh as a daisy and full of old buck. I thought of taking her along to our jitterbug soldiers and saying, 'This lady is spending a lot of her valuable time trying to teach you how to amuse yourselves. I cannot see why a person so obviously superior to you in every way should bother about the likes of you at all.' However, I didn't.

You may be right about Peter Alexander [who had just gone to the wars, and was later to become Professor of English at Glasgow University] but I don't think you quite fully appreciate that gallant warrior's side of it (or mine). No one can say of anyone else (except in the most general terms) what his duty is. I know that I hadn't the slightest shadow of doubt what mine was & I should think P.A. was the same. It is like following Jesus. The disciples no doubt had a devil of a time from their wives & families & all right thinking people & it is still doubtful whether they did what is called their duty — stravaiging about with tuppence in their pockets listening to the talk of a crazy man & doing no decent work & drinking & having a grand time while their boats & their cottages & their wives & kids were going all to pot. But they knew that, right or wrong, that was their way & some of them went the length of crucifixion on it . . . if everybody had been [living ordinary lives] there wouldn't have been any Hitler or Jesus or Genghis Khan or Pasteur or George Stevenson or Copernicus or James Watt or Shakespeare or Napoleon or Robespierre or Lenin & nothing would have happened except the steady

pressure of dull blackguards on top until the human race died
— at about 6000 B.C. — from inanition. I suppose there have
to be people who chance their arm & the welfare of all
their dependents because of some cracked idea that a certain
course of action is RIGHT. You, curiously enough, are more
likely to sympathise with them than most of your extremely
conservative sex. You are more than a bit of a mad apostle
& artist yourself. . . .

By early 1942, however, Mr Bridie was ready, panther-like, to
climb down from his tree and Major Mavor, who was after all
fifty-four, asked to be released from the army to return to his own
work. A letter to Tony Guthrie uses remarkably similar language
to that he used when he joined up:

> I have fallen out on to the Grass from the Oxter of
> the Tortoise, and largely (this disquiets me) by my own act.
> Thinking I should go mad, and disliking the idea, I pushed
> and pushed to get away from my Belfast Looney Bin, where
> I had comfort of a sort, safety, authority, agreeable company
> and daylong blessed idleness. I was an admirable King Log,
> and my frogs leapt about me and refrained from biting each
> other, for that is my particular and valuable mystery as a
> Commander. I railed also at Neo-Psychology in such good
> and continuous terms that my young men came down from
> their Cloud Cuckoo Land and did some very good work. . . .
> My first idea was a livelier job within the Army and one in
> which I should hate myself less. But my superiors lacked the
> ingenuity to find one for me, though they expressed the will
> to do so. Then a stupid brass hat annoyed me and I put in
> for compassionate release on the ground that I was one of
> the half dozen best dramatists in Britain and that the other
> five were doing excellent and patriotic work in plain clothes.
> After six weeks or so the War Office replied that this officer's
> release could not be approved without entailing inequity of
> treatment to other officers similarly situated. *What officers?*
> At about the same time an Army Council Instruction
> came out saying that officers over 45 and below the rank of
> Colonel were to have their cases reviewed and the old and
> doting were to be cast out. My immediate boss, knowing that
> I wanted to get out, put me up under this, washing, at the

same time, his hands of the whole matter. So I assembled in a sort of knacker's yard with a lot of other poor old boys and was interviewed by a distraught Brigadier wearing a V.C. ribbon and looking like Death warmed up. He gave me my ticket, and here I am.

The sole literary output of this period of over two years consists of a longish report he wrote for the Ministry of Information about Dublin, a film script about Burns which was not produced, and a short programme for the B.B.C. about J. M. Barrie which was. He returned to 'a hideous suburban Mansion' which Rona had bought in Bearsden, and started again.

13

On May 16th 1942 Mr Bridie wrote to Ian Dalrymple:

> I have not yet got orientated from the *dolce far niente* of
> Military Life. It is all very strange. . . . As to my part in this
> War Effort, it has not yet been revealed to me what it is to
> be. Blackburn [his agent for films] described scenes of
> unparalleled enthusiasm when he announced to the Film
> World that I was at their disposal, but no ripples of this
> enthusiasm have reached me so far. The Secretary of State
> of that locality informed me that All Scotland would at once
> leap to avail itself of my untrammelled genius, but so far it
> hasn't lep.
>
> So I have just sat down on my bottom (hypertrophied as
> it is in my Country's Service) and begun the composition of
> two great Exercises for the Classes of English Literature and
> Drama of 2100 A.D. or thereabouts. I've varied this by carting
> furniture — for Rona and I have moved into
> a hideous suburban Mansion and Rona has taken bronchitis
> and asthma and is unable to do the heavy work as she otherwise
> would have done. Robert and Bingo [Ronald] have gone back
> to school in Edinburgh till the Autumn when Robert will
> drift idly into H.M. Forces (I see from the papers that he
> took 4 wkts for 17 against the Royal Dick Veterinary College)
> and Bingo into the Study of Medicine.

I don't think the Bearsden house was all that hideous. I had
a nice room under the eaves and, like Gateside, the house stood
on a south-facing bluff at the end of a rather countrified lane. My
father described it to Guthrie:

It has a Lounge Hall with a bile-coloured fireplace & a bathroom linoleum roof. The drawing room was meant for a billiard room & has crossed billiard cues on the imitation mahogany roof. My room (which was the dining room) opens through a French window on a flight of steps leading from a red-tiled terrace with two huge terracotta-coloured cups on the balustrade. The whole front of the house is occupied by a blaes tennis court with green moss on it and a glass pavilion. Below that is a rock garden with a rotting pergola. Below that again is a little wood full of wood pigeons and rabbits.

It was to be home for four years — rather a long time by the Mavors' standards.

Reviving his pre-war career proved difficult. There were many false starts over *Susannah and the Elders*, and *Lancelot* proved almost more intractable. While on the Hospital Ship he had virtually sold it to Robert Donat, but when Donat quibbled about terms and, in the phrase of the time, reminded the author that there was a War on, he was sent one of Mr Bridie's most vehemently abusive letters, which he reserved exclusively for his friends.

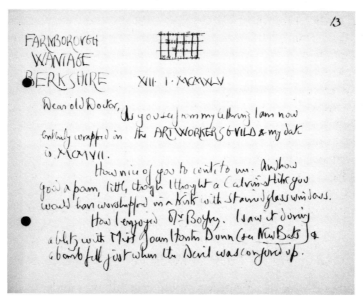

Excerpt from a letter of John Betjeman, 1945, mentioning a performance of *Mr Bolfry*. By permission of the Literary Executors of the Estate of John Betjeman.

CITIZENS' THEATRE

2ᵈ

IN THE ATHENÆUM, BUCHANAN STREET
(OPPOSITE BUCHANAN STREET SUBWAY)
NIGHTLY, MONDAY to SATURDAY at 7: SATURDAY MATINEES at 2
● UNDER THE AUSPICES OF C E M A

Programme for *Holy Isle*, the opening play by the Citizens' Theatre. The cover incorporates a device designed by Mavor. By permission of the Citizens' Theatre Ltd.

A few years later it was to be taken up, and indeed widely advertised, for production by the Old Vic in the great days when Olivier and Richardson had just come out of the Fleet Air Arm and played a famous season or two at the New Theatre. As late as 4th January 1945, John Burrell, the third member of the troika, was writing that the proposed production for March 20th had been postponed but that the Company would open their second season with it in Glasgow in April. They would later take it to New York. Mr Burrell admitted that this proposal 'deviates from the contract' but hoped Mr Bridie would agree. 'Tony [Guthrie],' he said, 'comes back on the 12th and will be getting cracking on *Lancelot* very soon after *Vanya* has opened on January 16th.'

It was not to be, and I think it was, at just the wrong moment, my father's biggest disappointment. Had he had a splendid production of this play with Olivier and Richardson, at the peak of their careers, much might have been different. At the time, however, he took it lightly. I remember the two shining lads coming to lunch in Bearsden and being very funny and charming; also a dinner in an unlicensed Glasgow restaurant — the Acropole, as I recollect — during which Richardson demanded coffee cups and kept filling them from a whisky bottle under the table. The plays they brought to Glasgow were, as I remember, *Peer Gynt*, *Henry IV, Part I* and *Arms and the Man*. My father wrote to Alastair Sim on April 23rd 1945:

Group at the opening of the Citizens' Theatre in its new premises.
Mrs Johnston, Rona Mavor, Walter Elliot, O. H. Mavor, Tom Johnston
(Secretary of State for Scotland). Reproduced from the *Bulletin*, 1945.

I have seen a little of the Flanagan and Allen of the Old
Vic. They broached the question of *Lancelot* in a sheepish
sort of way, saying that they had not put it on 'so far' because
of their growing and terrible misgivings about the lady they
had cast for Guenevere (absolutely against my wishes) — I
preserved a cold silence. . . .

I like Larry and Ralph very much, though I always feel
inclined to give them a bob for a poke of sweeties and some
ginger pop.

When the play was published Walter Elliot wrote:

You have done the trick and written the first of your Great
Plays, of which I hope there will be many more. But, for the
love of Mike, go on like your eminent predecessor, W. Shakespeare, in writing up stories first told you by someone else. I
do not know anyone in the world who can interpret a story
better or invent one worse.

Be that as it may . . . Mr Bridie was soon being sought out. In
November of 1942 he was asked to be the first Chairman of the
Scottish Committee of C.E.M.A. (the Council for the
Encouragement of Music and the Arts; later the Arts Council)
under Lord Keynes, and was very shortly busy about founding the

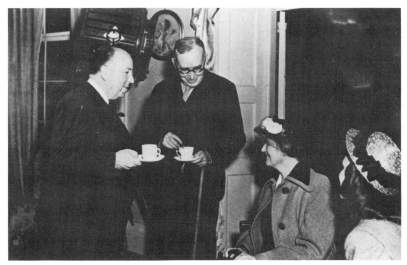

Alfred Hitchcock with the Mavors and their Canadian cousin, Sascha, on the set of *Under Capricorn*, 1948.

Glasgow Citizens' Theatre, of which he became the Chairman.

He was also writing plays and films. The film work was important to a man who had been supporting his family on army pay. He did a [Duke of] Marlborough film for Korda and then *The Paradine Case* for Hitchcock — little, if anything, of his work finally appearing (as is the way in that strange business) on the screen. He professed to prefer it that way. In 1946 he was asked to go to Hollywood for ten weeks to work on *Under Capricorn*, again for Hitchcock whom he liked and admired. He arrived in New York to find that Hitch had just left for London and, after a few comic episodes, tore up his contract and flew home. He completed the work in Bearsden.

The plays, however, were the thing, and he was soon in full production again. He wrote a charming little play, based on a story by Helen Waddell, whom he had met in Ireland, for the Pilgrim Players — a gallant bunch of actors under Martin Browne — who were touring worthy plays during the war: *The Dragon and the Dove*, which opened in September 1942. In December of that year, *Holy Isle* opened at the Arts Theatre in London, directed by — as he said in a letter to a friend — 'a pleasant maniac' called Alastair Sim. Sim had been in *What Say They?*, but this was to be the beginning of a very happy and productive period for both of them.

Alastair Sim, O. H. Mavor, and Robert Donat after the opening
performance of *It Depends What You Mean*. Reproduced from *Picture Post*,
4 November 1944.

Their next collaboration was over *Mr Bolfry*, a play about the
irruption of the Devil into a Highland manse. He appears, dressed
exactly like Mr McCrimmon, the minister, and delivers a sermon
in which, taking his text from William Blake, he commands his
tiny congregation to enjoy the Pride of the Eye and the Lust of
the Flesh, and to 'Let the Wild Horses loose!'. Naomi Sim — and
Alastair and Naomi were as near to having 'one soul in two bodies'
as you can get — has described in her marvellous book, *Dance and
Skylark*, how they objected to Bridie's original idea that the Devil
should turn out to be an escapee from the local asylum and demanded
a real Devil; whence the unaided exit of Bolfry's umbrella in the
last act and Mrs McCrimmon's, 'Och, well, dear me, a walking
umbrella's nothing to the queer things that happen in the Bible.
Whirling fiery furnaces and all these big beasts with the three heads
and horns. It's very lucky we are that it was no worse. Drink up
your tea'. And McCrimmon's, 'I have nowhere seen such great
faith, no, not in Israel'.

I can't forbear to quote one of Bernard Shaw's famous postcards.
It would seem that Dr Mavor had offered some medical advice in

Many thanks. I have noted the address; but at this moment it looks as if the patient were beyond all professional help. The end cannot be far off for either of us (she 86: I 87); but it seems very close now for the younger.

I saw the play at the Westminster, and remarked to Roy Limbert that I was glad to know that if I had nothing else for the drama I had at least made the production of such stunners as Bolfry possible. I enjoyed it all except the servant's part, of which not a word got across, because she had not been warned that dialect has to be articulated as clearly and artificially as blank verse. She thought only of imitating it successfully.

G. Bernard Shaw

4, WHITEHALL COURT, LONDON, S.W.I.

11th September 1943.

Letter of Bernard Shaw to Mavor, 1943. By permission of the Society of Authors on behalf of the Bernard Shaw Estate. © 1988 The Trustees of the British Museum, the Governors and Guardians of the National Gallery of Ireland and Royal Academy of Dramatic Art.

Scene from the original production of *The Forrigan Reel*. Photograph by J. F. Stevenson. Duncan Macrae, Helen Lacey, James Gibson.

the case of Mrs Shaw. The reply, so characteristic, is addressed, in that exquisitely legible hand, to Mr Bridie:

> Many thanks. I have noted the address; but at this moment it looks as if the patient were beyond all professional help. The end cannot be far off for either of us (she 86: I 87); but it seems very close now for the younger.

> I saw the play at the Westminster, and remarked to Roy Limbert that I was glad to know that if I had done nothing else for the drama I had at least made the production of such stunners as Bolfry possible. I enjoyed it all except for the servant's part, of which not a word got across, because she had not been warned that dialect has to be articulated as clearly and artificially as blank verse. She thought only of imitating it successfully.

G. BERNARD SHAW

Holy Isle and *Mr Bolfry* are, in a sense, complementary. In the former, a bunch of sophisticates come to a deserted island, muck it up, but leave it, at the end, inviolate. In *Bolfry* it is the Devil, himself, who visits a bein respectable household and is exorcised by Mrs McCrimmon and her pure and simple faith. It is interesting that they, and *The Forrigan Reel*, of December 1944, are set, uniquely, in the Highlands and Islands. The great Scottish hinterland is a kind of Arcadia to the urban Scot. Physically and metaphysically it is a place he can escape to where the air is fresher, the emotions purer, where the old plain men have rosy faces and the young fair maidens quiet eyes.

My father always valued this part of his heritage. I think he needed it at that time. In July 1944 Robert was killed in Normandy. It seems that his tank — he was a Lieutenant in the Lothians and Border Yeomanry — was sent out, shortly after they arrived west of Caen, to clear the area and was hit by an anti-tank gun. At first it was thought that the crew had escaped, but later evidence suggested that they were killed instantly. Robert had been the Golden Boy, but his death as far as I could see passed with a complete lack of expressed emotion, perhaps characteristic of the Glasgow bourgeoisie at the time.

In October 1944, Alastair Sim directed and played in *It Depends What You Mean*, at the Westminster, then run by Donat. In December the very young Citizens' Theatre in Glasgow presented *The Forrigan Reel*. Based on a story in a book of Highland Tales which Gordon Bottomley had sent to Bridie, it is about Mrs Grant of Forrigan who develops an obsession and thinks she is a clock. The great Duncan Macrae played a sheep-herd who cures her by dancing the moon up and down. He then cures a young English lady by a similar terpsichorean exercise.

Dr J. L. Halliday, the author of a remarkable book on *Social Medicine*, and a good friend, wrote a piece of penetrating psychological criticism of the play which deserves to be quoted in full. Dr Mavor, of course, thought it hilarious. I think it was as true as anything I have read about any Bridie play:

> Clearly the main theme of the play was mental suffering. This was announced in the Prologue in a sketchy form and the problem was worked out in the scenes which followed. In Act I (part of which seems to belong to an earlier period of

the author's life) the nature of the suffering was obsessional, intellectual preoccupation when the universe becomes dead and the living being automatic. Healing is achieved when the soul (female) makes contact with primitive natural healing forces, which are personified in the play by the chthonic characters of the dirty old man with the wisdom of the race and his son who is a 'natural'. In Act II the suffering includes physical disturbances when the body is racked by the emotions. Contemplation of this and the source of the suffering, reduces 'the company' to a state of whimpering impotence. Contact however is again made with the archaic healing forces and, although part of the soul (Mairi) mocks and then denounces the possibility, healing does take place and the soul and 'the company' are liberated — freed into life again, as expressed in the rhythm of the dance. In short, the problem is announced — mental suffering. A solution is sought and in the searching for this a true advance is made, leading to liberation. The advance and the solution are both emotionally reasonable. Thus FORRIGAN is the *real* thing . . . perhaps you had better not tell all this to Bridie because, as I see it now, he had very little to do with the play, which was written, contrived and accomplished mainly by Mavor himself. . . .

Whether or not Dr Halliday's analysis contains the truth of the matter, I see the plays of this period as a plunge into healing waters, as into a Highland stream running off the high tops in spring. The theme of all the plays is the recovery of innocence and, as Yeats wrote:

> How but in custom and in ceremony
> Are innocence and beauty born?

Like Yeats, both Dr Mavor and Mr Bridie believed in custom and in ceremony.

In the six years left to him, Mr Bridie was to attempt to develop this belief into a broader philosophy of life. There were nearly a dozen more plays to go.

14

The 1940s were a busy time. As Chairman of the Scottish
Committee of C.E.M.A. Bridie had to spend endless hours at
meetings in Edinburgh, London and elsewhere, helping to set the
plan whereby the Arts Council was, over the next twenty years,
to transform Britain from 'the land without music' to one of the
major centres of all the arts. But that is another story. When Keynes
died in 1946 and was replaced by Sir Ernest Pooley, no doubt an
admirable administrator but a civil servant who had been one of
the 'three blind mice' who exerted the censorship on behalf of the
Lord Chamberlain on stage plays, Bridie resigned.

But he was also busy, on a day-to-day basis, with the Citizens'
Theatre in Glasgow which opened on October 11th 1943, and
running a theatre is no picnic. I remember Stage Managers and
Board Members arriving at all hours to report on the latest crisis.
Bridie's description of the matter is typically low-key:

> After Artemus Ward's hero had languished in prison for
> several years, a happy thought struck him. He opened the
> window and got out. Starting a theatre is as easy as that.
>
> For years and years those of us who wanted a resident
> theatre in Glasgow had dug tunnels with rusty screwnails, had
> tamed mice and taught them to carry messages, had tried to
> saw through iron bars with dog-biscuits, had written our
> biographies on our shirts with blood, had implored the
> immortal gods — all to little or no purpose. Then six of us
> suddenly sat round a table and found it was quite easy. We
> asked a few other people for a little money and began.
>
> We took the little Athenaeum for a thirty weeks' season

Mavor outside the Citizens' Theatre during the run of A *Sleeping Clergyman*, 1947. By permission of the Citizens' Theatre Ltd.

and looked round for a producer. We were given a guarantee by C.E.M.A. to meet what we thought was an inevitable loss. It was war time. Actors were hard to come by and so was material. The theatre had a comfortable auditorium, but few other modern amenities. But two boards and a passion were enough. We broke even in our first year and made a four figure profit in our second. We did twenty plays and took two of them through Scotland to places ill-supplied with Drama. We hit a remarkably high standard of acting and production and chose no catchpenny plays. . . .

If the Scottish Theatre ever comes into being, I hope that we shall be a lively, efficient, experienced part of it and that we shall have some credit for producing, even at this early stage, a superior sort of article, honest in purpose and sound in workmanship.

The Athenaeum was in the basement of the then Royal Scottish Academy of Music and one emerged into blacked-out streets, but these were great days. I served briefly as an Assistant Stage Manager. Shortly Harry McKelvie gave Bridie the Princess's Theatre in the Gorbals — home of the most famous of the famous Glasgow pantomimes — for a tiny rent, and actors like James Gibson, Duncan Macrae, Jean Taylor Smith, Roddy Macmillan, Molly Urquhart, Andrew Keir, Fulton Mackay, Lennox Milne, Madeleine Christie, Stanley Baxter, Douglas Campbell and John Cairney — to name but a dozen — brought a new kind of vigour into the theatre and were to take it, by way of *The Thrie Estaites* at the Edinburgh Festival, to a wider public.

Bridie also founded the College of Drama, housed, like the Athenaeum, in the Academy of Music, and was one of the first group of people whom Harry Harvey Wood, then with the British Council, gathered to meet Rudolph Bing and work on his proposal for an Edinburgh Festival.

The Mavors continued their peripatetic life-style, moving first to a nicer villa in Bearsden with a view over the suburban railway — I remember Italian prisoners of war singing opera at their work — and then, in September 1947, to Drymen.

Finnich Malise was a delightful Georgian house with a view of Loch Lomond and 200 acres of land. The notion was to farm it, and a young manager was engaged. It seemed like a happy return to the idyllic days of Gateside. Lindsay Galloway and his wife returned to a tiny cottage on the grounds, and Jimmy Vickers's brother looked after the central heating. But it seemed that the land was, by some archaic Scotch law, let to a local farmer under what was called *tacit relocation* and a wearisome and prolonged law-suit gradually clouded the renewed pleasures of country life.

These were, however, considerable while they lasted. Rona and Osborne celebrated their twenty-fifth anniversary at one of many happy parties in the house. Osborne loved entertaining guests and Rona would drive them to Loch Lomond and the Trossachs, her husband singing hymns and psalms to alleviate the rigours of the journey. He was proposed for the Lord Rectorship of Glasgow University, which he would have loved, but was defeated by his old friend Walter Elliot. He enjoyed walking up the little Knockanhaglish Hill, above the house, and developed a method, suitable to his expanding figure and unathletic temperament, of destroying large weeds. He would clutch them between his boots and lean backwards, plucking them out of the damp moorland soil. We had a windmill to pump the water and I remember John Casson, who became Director of the Citizens' Theatre, standing on the fulcrum of the great wheel laughing with delight. It was my humble function to oil the thing, but I did it from several feet lower down. John, however, the son of Sir Lewis Casson and Dame Sybil Thorndike, had been at Dartmouth, and liked the exposure of wide open spaces.

The relationship with Alastair Sim was going extremely well. Alastair was rapidly becoming a major figure in films, but he loved the theatre, and he loved Bridie. I only got to know Alastair and Naomi well after my father's death, but I was able to see how marvellous and creative that relationship had been. *Dr Angelus*, based on the Glasgow murderer Dr Pritchard, which my father wrote for Alastair and George Cole, was very successful at the Phoenix Theatre, opening in July 1947, And *Mr Gillie* was still to come.

Naomi writes in her book:

> Those years during the Forties when the author/director-actor relationship between Jimmy [Bridie] and Alastair was going so well were exhilarating — something fresh always happening. When he came to London Jimmy would usually travel down by the night train and be already at the [Sims'] flat when I got up from the country. He would be rather quiet and reserved at first but the bar opened early for him, around 11 a.m., and after he'd had a drink it was as if another person entirely had come out from behind a curtain, talkative, enthusiastic, witty and a joy to be with.

I should, perhaps, add that my father's advice to me — often neglected — was that unless two drinks made you feel better, it was better to stop. On the whole, I think he lived by this rule.

Alastair, too, was a very abstemious man. The company, when they were together, was stimulation enough. It resulted in more than half a dozen plays, among the best achievements of both actor and author.

When Alastair died, in 1976, I wrote about him, and have not much to add to what I wrote then:

He was for over a dozen years the closest colleague — one could as well say collaborator — of my father, the playwright James Bridie, and I had the privilege of having him act in my own play *A Private Matter* three years ago.

Neil Gunn wrote of Bridie that 'he was the only man who ever made me feel that literature — writing — was a ploy, an adventure in common, like poaching, not a "serious" business but a foray in delight'.

This was absolutely true of the Bridie-Sim association. . . .

In spite of associations with William Golding, Michael Gilbert and William Trevor over a number of plays, and two late big successes in Pinero plays, Alastair Sim never quite recaptured the, to him, necessary ambience, the sense of 'a foray in delight' which that period had provided. But in the cinema he went from strength to strength and his became one of the best known faces in the world.

Paradoxically he was the most private of men. He was simply uninterested in the trappings of fame and had a positive horror of publicity, not only because he didn't like it, but also from a good Scotch puritanical conviction that it was evil and corrupting.

He would never have forgiven me the word 'puritanical'. Anything to do with gods and god-men was anathema. People were good enough for him and, in particular, he drew confidence from the ability of the human race to keep on producing new human beings with new ideas. The young, he thought, were always right — in principle. He might find it necessary to correct some of their misapprehensions — but these would be misapprehensions inculcated by adults. And if any of the young should prove a disappointment, no matter, there would be more and younger young coming up any minute. There is a great deal of Alastair Sim in 'Mr Gillie', the schoolteacher whose swans turn out to be only geese, but who doesn't lose faith in them. . . .

There is a much-quoted remark [from his Rectorial Address at Edinburgh] that Alastair Sim realised he was a fool and lived happily ever after. This could be misunderstood. On 'this great stage of fools' he was quite clear that no one should have the pretension to think himself anything else. But he did not opt out. Seeing him rehearse a role in a play was to see a great artist, and a great clown, at work. And the secret, as in all the performing arts, perhaps all the arts, is to care enough: to care enough about those three words, that gesture, really to work at it and get it right. Of course, one must also have the vision to know what right is.

He always, and only a few weeks ago, ticked me off for forcing my own ideas on to the characters in a play. I was usurping the characters' own right to their own independent points of view. 'I hate to hear the author speaking through a play,' he said. And when we were rehearsing A Private Matter he would again and again argue that during such and such a speech one of the other characters must be reacting in such and such a way. 'Yes, it's a serious speech,' he would say, 'but can't you see, Anthony thinks it's a load of rubbish!'

This is crucial. As it was the endlessly renewing remarkableness of the human race that inspired his life and its work, so, at the end of the day, it was each individual's autonomy that gave cause for hope. The characters he played and the plays he directed celebrated the individual's right to be himself; not to be larger than life, but to be life lived up to its potential. And this didn't mean pushing people around; it meant cherishing them. He was a wise man.

The influence of Sim on Bridie, and vice-versa, was immensely to their mutual benefit. There was, however, a part of Mr Bridie which — however 'Jimmy' delighted in the Simian forays — wanted to write the 'Great Play' and have it performed by, however much he hated them, the leading managements. This was before the days of the National Theatre and the Royal Shakespeare's current magnificence.

This part of Mr Bridie wasn't doing quite so well.

He had written in 1946 a play, based on the 14th and 15th books of the Iliad which he called Old Nobility. It was about Gods and Men (the only proper alternative to Love and Honour) and all kinds of plans were discussed for Guthrie to direct it for H. M. Tennent, then the leading London producer, with Fay Compton or Edith Evans or whoever. . . . He also wrote John Knox, which

Scene from *The Queen's Comedy* at Edinburgh, 1950. Photograph by
J. F. Stevenson. By permission of the Citizens' Theatre Ltd.

was about Love and Honour, and the Old Vic were going to
present it at the first Edinburgh Festival, but found it 'too Scotch'.
These were disappointments, although Guthrie finally directed *The
Queen's Comedy*, as it was then called, at the Edinburgh Festival
in 1950, and *John Knox* had a certain *succès d'estime* or *de scandale*
when the Citizens' Theatre performed it with John Laurie in the
lead, and Scottish writers from Hugh MacDiarmid to Eric Linklater
filled the Glasgow newspapers with furious debate.

There was compensation, however, when Olivier produced
Daphne Laureola at the Wyndham's Theatre in March 1949 with
Edith Evans and a young actor called Peter Finch, whom he had
recently discovered in Australia and who was making his debut on
the London stage.

The Queen's Comedy showed a Jupiter who, after the tragedies
of the Trojan War, attempted to explain to the suffering mortals
that 'he had not nearly finished his Great Experiment and that
"there was plenty of time" '. *John Knox* showed two major historical
figures, the other being Mary Queen of Scots, who, at the end,

regretted that they had been so taken up with the importance of their disparate *weltanschauungs* that they had forgotten how to be just people. *Daphne Laureola* is set on the edge of a pit, due to London bombing, and a remarkable lady enchants and inspires a young Polish student and then rejects him, and, on the death of her rich husband, marries her chauffeur-cum-keeper. It has echoes of the first play, *The Switchback*, with its talk of dying civilisations:

> It always happens. 'An hundred generations, the leaves of autumn, have dropped into the grave.' And again we shiver miserably in the confines of a long winter as christendom and the Roman Empire did hundreds of years ago. Again and again and again we have covered the face of the earth with order and loveliness and a little justice. But only the face of it. Deep down below the subterranean brutes have bided their time to shake down our churches and palaces and let loose the little rats to sport among the ruins.

Guthrie was, typically, critical and wrote, before the production:

> The soliloquys of Lady P. [to be played by Edith Evans] and the death of the old boy are *masterly* — absolutely corking, first-rate, top notch stuff.
>
> *What* a poet you could be if you weren't such a goddamned *amateur*. Now do *please* tussle with this piece and make it your chef d'oeuvre. It has all the ingredients you need — characters, atmosphere (highly contemporary) and a theme. But I don't believe you've really decided what it's about — on the conscious plane what you really *mean* it to be about; or (arguing from analogy — and you know plenty about the Human Beast) what, on the conscious plane, it's really about. The script is now in shape for you to *begin* work.

I don't know what alterations were, or were not, made. In the event Bridie was pleased with the final production and wrote to Ian Dalrymple on March 28th 1949:

> It was a honey of an evening. I don't know how much it owed to what must be the greatest comedy actress who ever lived; how much to a really first rate production by Murray Macdonald, and how much to the members

of a really good cast, from whom I single out Peter Finch.

And, three months later, in a characteristic letter from the Marine Hotel, North Berwick:

> Your letter has given me that agreeable sense that J.C. must have felt when Auld Hornie took him to the high place and showed him the Cities of the World. Get thee, however, behind me, Satan. The production was as good as I or anybody else could get in London. The set was another matter, but that is another story. The Dame proved herself a world champion at 66. (Mind you, the part is cast iron and I long to see a repertory or amateur actress in it and, perhaps, the play might gain by the absence of an actress eighteen feet high.) Anyhow, you have never seen any more wonderful acting. . . .
>
> I am with you about Master Finch. The only other man who has appreciated his achievement is A. Sim, and I think he is right. I love the public, and am their humble servant, but couldn't they, or one of their fuglemen in the Press, have seen that he was forcing them to see the whole thing through his eyes? This was right, and what I meant; but it was a Hell of a job in the face of Edith's obvious blazing brilliance.
>
> May I tell you what happened since I began this letter? Miss Steele, a young Englishwoman who looks like an underdone beef steak, came into the room to arrange the flowers. She does it for nine hours a day in this pub. So I asked her if anybody had offered her a glass of sherry in token of their appreciation of her artistry. She said, 'No.' So I gave her what I thought was a glass of sherry, but which turned out to be a glass of neat whisky. She didn't know the difference, but I had to change it (I don't drug young women for my own evil purposes) and that meant that I had to drink two neat whiskies, and that after my aperitif and my pint (for it is just after lunch) so there you are. I could go on for ever. . . .

His old mentor, Ayliff, who had recently written that, 'you and G.B.S. are the only gods of my acquaintance without feet of clay', wrote, just before his death:

Edith Evans as Lady Pitts and Peter Finch as Ernest Piaste in *Daphne Laureola*. Reproduced from *Theatre World*, June 1949. By permission of *Plays and Players*.

Daphne Laureola by J. Bridie, Apothecary and Genius. You didn't ask me for my opinion of the above; so here it is: — Yes, it's a lovely play; not so meaty as *The Clergyman* but with much more pure beauty.

And this I will maintain at the point of my tongue in Clubs and places where they talk nonsense, in spite of the fact that, in my seat in the sixth row of the stalls, I didn't hear 20% of the dialogue. Why does Mother Melpomene decree that her most favoured children should be seen but not heard. . . .

Edith is quite beautiful in Act I. So beautiful, in fact, that the effect of it sustained me through the slipping away of her performance in Act II and the lamentable inaudibility in the big speech downstage in Act III. I knew it was the big speech because of the necessity for it at that point, and from the glimmers of brilliance that reached me whenever she forgot she was a Dame of the B.....h Empire and let herself be the fine, honest to goodness actress she is. . . . Damn her, she's been blessed with a voice like the Last Trump; why must she go and wrap it in a napkin and hide it in the pit of her stomach?

P.S. Did I mention that *Daphne Laureola* was a lovely play?

Three months after the opening of *Daphne Laureola* the Mavors moved again, this time to Craigendoran, near Helensburgh, on the Clyde coast.

15

'Sewage View' was a noble old house dating from the days when the Glasgow merchant princes built their palazzos down the Clyde coast. It was not far from Kilcreggan, where Osborne had spent his summers half a century before, and maybe not far from his invented 'Shults' or 'Baikie'.

He had begun *The Baikie Charivari* at Finnich Malise, and it was not to be performed until after his death. It is based upon Punch and Judy, that great folk epic which, in my youth, one might suddenly find being performed, in its grandfather-clock-like red-and-white tent in the West End Park. Sir James Pounce-Pellott — and Punch is popularly believed to owe some heredity to Pontius Pilate, that other celebrated ritual murderer, and representative of authority — has been a worthy District Commissioner in India. He returns, in his retirement, to 'Baikie' on the Clyde coast and humbly invites such locals as he meets — each of them a Punch and Judy character — to inform him about the modern world which has replaced that which he knew. As Bridie says in his Prefatory Note: 'The sun may have set on the British Empire, but do let us make use of the afterglow to read the Book of Fate.' At the end Pounce-Pellott — and it is not a realistic play — symbolically murders all the false prophets and confronts the Devil himself. Like Peer Gynt with the Button Moulder he wins a reprieve and concludes that all he can do is 'jest again and await my reply . . .' Like *The Switchback* it is a Morality Play. Like Dr Mallaby, Pounce-Pellott has the guts to go on.

The move, after Drymen, to even earlier roots was not proving a success. My father wrote to Ian Dalrymple in March 1949:

O. H. Mavor and Eric Linklater by Anton Wasilewski. Reproduced from
the *Sketch*, 30 August 1950.

Rona and I are having one Hell of a time. We have bought
the above expensive house in Helensburgh, have filled it with
painters, joiners and plasterers and have decided to sell it
again. We are staying in a temperance hotel, but move shortly
into our ruin with two camp beds and a picnic basket. I am
getting too old for this sort of thing.

I am afraid Rona is right about Helensburgh. It has become
rather a squalid den since I knew it last. . . . We are now
looking for a furnished house with a long let till we can find
a proper place to live. As laundries here are very deliberate,
we are getting rather filthy and smelly. To say nothing of
ill-tempered.

Would you like me to write you a realistic film, full of the
sordidness and frustration of life? Not that I shall be able to
do it, as I have no secretary and no books and find it difficult
to write in temperance hotel bedrooms. . . .

Eighteen months later they had bought a lovely seventeenth-
century house east of Edinburgh — 'It is about ten miles due
South from North Berwick and has got four ghosts' — but Rona
was to move into it alone. The Craigendoran house, bang on the
edge of the Clyde with a pretty night view of the lights of Port
Glasgow and Greenock across the river, was, for all its faults, their
last home. Pounce-Pellott's opening aria in *The Baikie Charivari*
goes: 'They still shine across the wine dark waters, the late lamps

of Port Girning and Plannock. They'll soon be drowned in the grey of another dubious dawn', whereupon he whistles a few bars of 'e lucevan le stelle' from *Tosca*.

Walter Elliot, and Winifred Bannister in her *James Bridie and his Theatre*, suggest that Bridie felt he had come to the end of his playwriting. I'm not sure about this. He was tired, certainly, and I remember visiting — when I was working at a hospital south of the river — and thinking 'You poor old man: you are going to die'. And, although there is a temptation to read *any* writer's last works as, to a greater or lesser extent, valedictory, what is certain is that he was still bubbling with ideas and projects.

It is true that he dedicated the last play to be published in his lifetime, *Mr Gillie*, to his old masters in what might well be read as a farewell gesture, 'In memory of JOHN BRANDANE, W. G. FAY and H. K. AYLIFF', and over these last plays there hangs a gentle gloaming glow; but I don't believe he would ever have stopped writing plays, had he not died at the age of sixty-three.

In 1948 Bridie had been interested in a story about theatre wars in Glasgow. The small local theatres in the mid-nineteenth century were known as 'penny geggies' and the character of J. J. Alexander, who ran one of these, seemed a good part for Sim.

23rd July 1948

Some time ago I told you about the notion I had for a play about a geggie proprietor. It has come up again, but now I want it to be a film. Do you know anything about the theatre war in Glasgow in the 1840's? I don't know very much about it myself but at one stage there were two theatres on separate floors of the same building and the lower theatre put up smoke in its transformation scenes that came through the floor and made the top audience cough, and the top theatre put on a grand water scene that drookit the patrons below. A fight followed.

I have also a theory that both 'Romeo and Juliet' and 'Troilus and Cressida' are plays about theatre wars in London. There may be some doubts about 'R and J' but none about 'T and C' which is obviously about actors and their gang warfare, which was more forthright and direct in those days than in ours.

Well, then. I write a new 'Romeo and Juliet' with you and

Barry Fitzgerald as Montagu and Capulet, and your daughter falling in love with Barry Fitzgerald's leading juvenile. What about it?

He returned to the subject on September 3rd in a letter written in a style he sometimes adopted for the Sims with no punctuation or capital letters. It is written in the middle of the second Edinburgh Festival in which Guthrie had had a great success, with the Glasgow Citizens' Theatre Company, in a revival of the mediaeval Scots play *The Thrie Estaites*.

> at north berwick i had a long talk or two with ian dalrymple with whom i made storm in a teacup long long ago like the bells of evening pealing he is very good and a gentleman and he is going to make that film i told you i had in my head about the theatre wars in glasgow about the middle of last century
>
> you hummed and hawed when i told you but do please come into this it will be really good . . .
>
> it has not yet got much of a shape and wont have till a respectable sum of money is put to my bank account but i give you my word of honour as a gentleman that it will be the best film ever made in Britain so hum not and haw not but come into it blind partly to please me and partly for the hell of it
>
> by the way guthrie wants to direct it ill take another page to tell you about that side of the situation guthrie and dalrymple and i had lunch in edinburgh in the royal suite of the n b guthrie is very keen but he may be doing some bloody opera or something and satyre of the three estaits is a raging, tearing, walloping success i think you and larry are splendid producers but neither of you is up to guthrie's kneecap on his day and by god monday before last was guthries day . . .

Sim replied on September 4th:

> Of course I'm with you blind and up to the ears. If I hummed and hawed it was only because I did not believe that Hitchcock would play with the Bridie-Sim ball. But I'm all for Guthrie. Even as a stage producer he has us all licked, except only where the understanding of Bridie character, situation, subtlety and diabolism is concerned. In that realm I stand

Alastair Sim and Ronald Adam in *Mr Gillie*, 1950. Photograph by Houston Rogers. By permission of The Raymond Mander & Joe Mitchenson Theatre Collection.

supreme and utterly alone and you bloody well know it. But the making of films is a mystery beyond my ken and only when a God is persuaded to copulate with a Robot do you get a good one. I believe this to be well within Tony's capabilities and I'm all for placing our filmic destinies in his hands.

I wish I could see his production in Edinburgh, but I may have to start a film next week. Try to have yours ready by the time I'm through, then all out for Punch and Judy. After that you can have a short rest.

And in early September:

> I have to face it. Everything that comes my way seems to turn my stomach, everything, that is, except the products of my old and much afflicted friend: James (God bless-sim) Bridie. Archie Batty [by then Bridie's agent with Curtis Brown] has phoned me and deeply bayed at me in a moving appeal to take over the Georgie Wood scheme [to rent the Westminster theatre for a repertory of plays], to sink all petty differences and return to give the Bridie productions the dignity they deserve. Through my tears I explained that we had never had any differences which mere mortals could understand and that great spirits like ours must always wait on Destiny.
>
> All the same I'm prepared to give Destiny a gentle kick on the backside by doing The Anatomist, if you would like me to and I can get the right cast. . . . [He did.]

Thereafter there was *Mr Gillie*, again with George Cole, which opened at the Garrick in February 1950. On September 22nd, Bridie wrote:

> Eileen Beldon sent me a cutting — I think from the *Telegraph* — about the Mayor of Vaucluse-la-Fontaine who was badgered by Communists on his Town Council. He passed a by-law banning the atom bomb in his commune (which contained eight hundred and twenty-six inhabitants) and instructed the village policeman to arrest anybody who brought an atom bomb into the neighbourhood or erected a cyclotron.
>
> Do you think it would be pleasant to put the French commune somewhere in Galloway or in the Highlands, and would you like to play the Mayor?

J. B. Priestley, in his generous Introduction to Bridie's posthumous *Meeting at Night*, writes:

> In November 1950 . . . I crossed the Clyde to stay yet again with Bridie. We had to discuss a scheme for sharing a famous old theatre, with a new play each and two stars, during the 1951 Festival [of Britain] season. He had been ill, I knew, but now seemed better, and we motored around, staring at

the old liners waiting to be broken up, we played billiards, we sat up and talked. Only one thing was new, strange, sad: I could not make him catch fire about the 1951 scheme; and soon, bewildered, beginning to feel something was wrong, I said no more about it. And when I understood why he cared no longer, I was in the wrong place. Two months later I was in Arizona when the news came he was dead and, with nobody to talk to who would understand what that meant, I went to my bungalow, opened the only bottle of good Scotch for miles and miles, and shared it with my memory of him. And ever since, I feel, the Theatre has seemed only half the size, half the fun, it used to be.

Of course, one doesn't want to revise a genuine and heartfelt tribute of that kind. My father's letter to Alastair Sim, however, is not readily open to so fatalistic an interpretation. It reads:

> I have just had an almost two-day session with Priestley. He was full of persuasion and eloquence about a scheme he and Binkie and Ralph Richardson have in mind for the Festival of Britain. I suppose it is very private and confidential and I know that you will regard it as such; but I thought I had better let you know about it.
>
> Binkie is prepared to take the Haymarket for eight or ten weeks during the height of the Festival and to put on two plays in repertory (yet to be written) by Priestley and me, the stars to be Ralph and Edith Evans. . . .
>
> I told him that I had a play for you at the top of my priority list . . . . I don't think much of the scheme, though the Haymarket is a nice theatre. I conceded to him that if I had an unexpected rush of energy and inspiration I might write two plays before May, but that I did not think it at all likely. . . .

To which Sim replied characteristically:

> Your letter didn't make much sense to me. I really can't be bothered very much with Priestley, though I admit he has occasional visitations from a demi-semi-god. Also, you know that I am not inflamed with the Festival spirit. It enhances only the glitter and tends to obscure what may be inside, and, as you know, I am a hell of a fellow for trying to get inside.

Your last paragraph was the one I read with delight. So let's just you write the first draft and me read it and go on from there in the time-honoured way. . . . . It looks very like as if I am going to do Scrooge. . . .

Bridie's last letter to Sim, dated January 7th 1951 — he was to die three weeks later — was written just after he had emerged from his old hospital:

I forget whether I told you that I have been having a Merry Xmas & H.N.Y. in the Victoria Infirmary with a choked deep vein in my leg. I am now out but not at large.

This morning I had an IDEA. You are probably too much of a blooming funk to do it. If so, I shall give it to Larry. Did I tell you he wrote from his tramp steamer begging me for a play for Vivien?

The idea is a character founded on Beaverbrook (round about 1800) who gets his knife in a little hack writer and chases him about in the most fantastic way with the final idea that he will make his fortune. Just as he is about to do this, the little man shoots him. There is a part for either Celia Johnson or Vivien Leigh.

In December Osborne and Rona had a short holiday at their old watering-hole, the Marine Hotel in North Berwick — presumably also having a look at Ruchlaw, the house they had just bought in East Lothian. On the way back to Glasgow Rona had persuaded Osborne to have a check-up with his old friend and colleague Sir James Learmonth, Professor of Surgery at Edinburgh. Shortly after leaving the hospital Osborne felt very ill and Rona turned the car and drove him back to the Royal Infirmary.

I was then working, as a doctor, at the American Hospital in Paris. Learmonth sent me a telegram saying: 'Your father has had a subarachnoid haemorrhage [bleeding into the covering of the brain]. He is in satisfactory condition but I think you should come'. When I got to the hospital my father was hallucinating. 'The lights are all on in Nineveh,' he said. He recognised me and asked what the hell I was doing there. After a few days he seemed better and he was transferred to Sir Derek Dunlop's medical wards. There he fell out of bed and, presumably, had a further bleeding. On our last visit my mother and I met Dr Alec Glen and Dr Bryce

O. H. Mavor and J. B. Priestley at the Malvern Festival, 1938.

McCall Smith in the corridor, his old friends from Baku and the Victoria Infirmary. They said he was very far through, but that they had brought him a wee dram, as it always cheered him up. We paid a brief visit and were phoned at the North British Hotel that evening by Learmonth to say that he had died.

I want to quote the last letter which he received from Tyrone Guthrie, his oldest friend in the theatre and severest critic. It was written on 24th December. Bridie died at the end of January. The references are to the proposed revival of *The Thrie Estaites* for the Edinburgh Festival and to Guthrie's play *Top of the Ladder* which had been running in London with John Mills in the lead:

> This will arrive late for the feast: none the less Greetings.
>
> I nipped up to Glasgow last week to see John Casson and get things a wee bit tidier about 3 *Estates*, and was so sorry to hear you were again bedded. This brings our joint and most affectionate wishes for your speedy recovery; and sympathy to Rona who must be having rather a dreary Xmas.
>
> Is there *anything* I can do to be useful, stimulating, soothing, uplifting, debasing, or what? There just *might* be some quelquechose that one could attend to on your behalf in this Babylon. If so you have but to say the word — my capacity is limited but energy *great*, and can be wholly at your service till Jan. 3. But you *don't* need to think of bothering to reply. . . .
>
> Top-Ladder comes off on Dec. 30. I shall be glad. It worries me to think of it going on there and losing a lot of money. It's a sad fact that a play simply has to be A Success — the theatre is a sort of party, and when it doesn't 'go' it's embarrassing and miserable for one and all. One absolutely knows that whether it 'goes' or not depends on all sorts of factors other than the merit of the play. But that doesn't prevent a feeling of embarrassment at the continuance of unwanted rites — *what* timbrels and *what* dances and what a scanty and inattentive congregation!
>
> Best of wishes from us both, always.
>
> T.

16

The Conversation with Oliver Goldsmith in Heaven (related in an earlier chapter) from *One Way of Living* continues:

> Things had come to pass. I had written plays and been paid for them. The facts of the case were now in the comfortable, intelligible, malleable Past. I was prepared to speak up to Goldsmith as a tradesman of his craft.
>
> There was nobody there. I took up my story sadly and it was dull, dreadfully dull. This great adventure, this Sindbadism of the Soul was no more lively a matter than collecting passports and tickets and insuring the luggage. . . .

For most of my life I was prepared to agree that after, say, his return from Baku in 1919 my father's life *was*, although full of triumphs and disasters on the stage, lacking in much more lively matters than dates and productions and the writing of yet more plays. And I incline to agree with Anthony Burgess who once said that the biography of an artist *is*, quite simply, the record of his works. 'A good biographer must explicate preoccupations of plot and style, and worry about symbols.' This is not, of course, what I have attempted here.

On the other hand I find *false* the notion of my father as a eupeptic, lazy, happy dilettante in the theatre, whose plays came from an abounding enjoyment of life. He did enjoy life, and all his friends pay tribute to that enjoyment and to his ability to share it. It bubbles from his plays, and there is not one of them which has not delighted audiences, made them laugh, shown them their fellows in a light such as to engage their sympathy and understanding for the Human Comedy. If I have painted a darker picture it is partly because, a third of a century after his death, I think there is a danger of his works disappearing under the harsh glare of contemporary fashion, as the lines of an old print fade into the paper, leaving only a pinchbeck pattern of roseate clouds. Mr Bolfry, the Devil returned to wartime Scotland, illustrated the point by referring to Mr McCrimmon's engraving of 'the worthy Dr Scanderlands of Fetterclash':

> The portrait was bitten into a plate with acid and printed in ink on paper. . . . Would you recognise it as the Doctor if it were all black ink or white paper? . . . neither you nor I nor anyone else can tell anything about Heaven or Hell, or this very imperfect makeshift of an earth on which we stand, without our blacks and our whites and our greys, which are whites mixed with black.

Bridie, who had survived two wars and had seen much of the Devil and His works, was much more the Stoic than the Epicurean, more black lines than pink clouds.

It is significant that the other playwrights mentioned by Dr Goldsmith in the Conversation are, with the exception of Schiller (the son of a surgeon and himself, as we would say, a 'paramedic'), qualified medical practitioners: Chekhov and Maugham.

The physician, by the nature of his profession, meets people at the extreme. Their sorrows fill his day. But he has to keep a part of himself from sharing these sorrows. He has to retain an ironical aspect of himself — and irony is the very yeast of drama — so that, to the patient, he is a rock in a wild sea. This is the secret of Chekhov's unassailable conviction that his plays were comedies, even farces, while Stanislavsky believed them to be tragedies. Hence, too, Walter Elliot's remark about a 'pitiless' quality in his old friend. One can, must, love one's fellow men. One is not asked to agree with them about the awfulness of their predicaments. It is possible, perhaps necessary, to take an ironic view, even to be an optimist. The deserts of Palmyra, the subterranean brutes, are waiting, and have the time to wait, to let loose the little rats which will sport among the ruins of our civilisation. On the other hand, who knows, there may be a God and He, too, presumably has plenty of time in which to work out His purpose.

The plays, of course, are the thing.

Since Bridie died they have — as is often the way with the works of writers — been somewhat neglected in a theatre which has embraced Socialist Realism and a dozen other -isms. The tender flame has been gallantly kept alive by Kenneth Ireland at Pitlochry and, more recently, by Tom Fleming and the Scottish Theatre Company. I confess that I have not been too unhappy about the general neglect, because I have a hunch that the plays as they were perceived to be in my father's lifetime are not the *real* plays. I think they are, not all of them, but more than a handful, due to be rediscovered.

In a recent essay in the *New York Review of Books* (March 1988), Jonathan Lieberson writes of Chekhov (another doctor/dramatist): 'He was accused of having no philosophy and of offering no universal "solutions" to the social, political, and other human problems of his time. But one suspects that he had no "philosophy of life" because he knew that none was adequate. . . . Most human problems are not amenable to the kind of all-purpose solutions we look for, Chekhov suggests.'

And William James, having detected in himself the 'feverish personal ambition' to 'settle the Universe's hash in one more book', wrote: 'Childish idiot — as if formulas about the Universe could ruffle its majesty, and as if the common sense world and its duties were not eternally the really real!' My father would have agreed with both writers.

Yet, what timbrels, what dances! How marvellously he turned to mirth all things of earth as only boyhood (normally) can! And, although his upbringing and background made him, above all, a moral playwright, how well he loved his fellow men, and women, and strove to show them as tender, suffering, infinitely gentle, and funny.

> Listen to this. 'She came downstairs. She went to an office and sat there all day. She went back to her divan room at six-thirty and stayed there reading library novels. She had no friends and no money to spend.' . . . If I make her alive then I have told a story, a story you can round off with your own moral. If I put a murder in the next flat, a love affair with her employer or any such miserable incident I put it in because otherwise no one would buy this story. But they are not the story. The story is the girl herself, coming to life, reaching to you over the footlights and telling you that you are not alone in the world; that other human beings live, suffer, rejoice and play the fool within the same limitations that bind you. . . .

Neil Gunn and O. H. Mavor, 1949. Photograph by Lida Moser from
Vogue, 1950. © The Condé Nast Publications Ltd.

This was what he had to say. This was what he had to say 'on God's behalf'. And if it didn't add up to a philosophy, or to a solution to the problems of the world, it was the communication of one who had seen a good deal of the world, and of the Devil, but who chose — unlike many of our wild lads of today — not to 'let the wild horses loose' and to respect, even love, the day-to-day triumphs and disasters of his fellow men for whatever they are worth.

The Ultimate Judge in *Mr Gillie*, in spite of the village schoolmaster's apparent non-success in his life, promotes him to a vacant seat between Lincoln and John Wesley:

> I find that this man devoted his life to opening cages and letting prisoners fly free. It was not his fault if the cat got the prisoners in the end. . . . I find most good men occupied in designing and strengthening cages. I do not like cages. I think that the minutes between the door of the cage and the jaws of the cat make life worth living.

In nearly forty plays James Bridie celebrated the human spirit. His earlier wrestlings with his duties, functions and demands as an artist, give way to a wider anxiety, about how to forgive the world its awfulness, to cherish its richness, to justify God's ways to man. It was not an unworthy vocation.

If our more recent age has preferred extravagance, has preferred to go the whole hog, to demand, in an absurd universe, a total freedom existentially to choose and do whatever the impulse dictates, this may not be the end of the story. To choose a personal freedom, and Devil take the consequences, is not necessarily the right, or the hardest, choice. Osborne Mavor's heredity, and his experience, taught him the virtues of a morality which, in recent years, has been largely rejected, worse, has become unfashionable. I have tried to suggest that that morality sprang not from idleness or even from an innate conservatism, but was forged in a white-hot fire. Yes, had he cast it off he might have written the one great play of which he was capable — and which I think he did not achieve — as O'Neill, with a quarter of his talent in invention, in wit, in verbal felicity, *did* write *Long Day's Journey Into Night* and *The Iceman Cometh*, destroying three wives and two children along the way. But, again, what timbrels, what dances!

And may not a happier age rediscover a writer whose humanity, whose wit, whose gentle humour, whose range, even whose morality will speak to them words of comfort and encouragement in the difficult task of being human?

Gabriel Marcel, the French philosopher and critic, was to write (in *Etudes Anglaises*, Oct.-Dec. 1957):

> Comment ne saurait-on pas à Bridie le gré le plus vif . . .
> d'avoir ainsi proclamé avec une espèce d'alacrité joyeuse les
> droits imprescriptibles de la personne et de l'effort créateur?
>
> [How can one fail to have the keenest sense of gratitude
> towards Bridie . . . for having thus proclaimed with a sort of
> happy alacrity the inalienable rights of the individual and of
> the creative spirit?]

I cannot think of a better way to end this brief account of my father's life, in which, as Walter Elliot said, 'He was full-blown when he originated. I remember him almost exactly the same when he was a schoolboy', than by quoting a letter to Arthur Wallace, he who, almost half a century before, had brought back the song 'Ygorra' to Glasgow University and to those who went to that earlier war. I think the letter, written within barely half a year of his death, represents the Bridie, and the Mavor I think *I* knew, better than any other text. It refers, like Dr Halliday's letter on *The Forrigan Reel*, to the 'primitive natural healing forces' still to be found in the Scottish countryside. It shows his delight in his fellow men. It celebrates custom and ceremony.

> I went last week to the Hawick Common Riding. It was
> one of the most exciting things I have ever seen or heard.
> Have you been there?
>
> It is, of course, the Green Man in The Golden Bough,
> riding through the town to bring in the leafing of the oak. They
> even wear oak leaves. Ostensibly it celebrates the Hornshole
> battle, the year after Flodden, when the halflins of Hawick
> rode out on the plough horses and beat an English raiding
> party and brought back the Hexham Abbey flag.
>
> I had to give the 'oration' at the Colour bussing. I cried
> like a cow and could hardly get through my speech.
>
> The town hall and the streets outside were packed and
> they had loudspeakers for the people who couldn't get in. The
> Cornet's followers in the gallery facing the platform sang like
> Hell for an hour before we arrived. Then the fife band came

Ceremony at the Hawick Common Riding, 1950. Far left: Lady Elliot
with O. H. Mavor. By permission of the Tweeddale Press Group.

up the middle aisle to lead in the Provost and his Bailies in
their red gowns. I used to think fifes sounded like piddling
in biscuit tins but, when they play Teribus, they are really
spirit-stirring all right.

They went out and came in again leading the Cornet's
Lass and her attendants, all dressed up to the nines. Then
the Macer gave the colours to a maid-of-honour, who pushed
them up through crossed halberds to the Lass (vide JURGEN),
who tied a favour to the flag and then handed it to the
Provost, saying that it had been well and truly bussed. The
Provost said, 'Thank you, Gracie', and the band came back
with the Cornet, between his green-coated Right Hand and
Left Hand Man.

The Lass hung on his sash and the Provost gave him the
flag and ordered him to carry it round the Marches. He said
he would, with great brevity and dignity. He is a bar boy by
profession.

I then made a really bloody awful speech and several songs
were sung, including the excellent PAWKIE PAITTERSON'S AULD
GREY YAUD; finishing up with TYR HAEBBE US TYR Y ODIN.

146

The leader sings the first two lines of each stanza and the audience take up the second two lines and then slap into the chorus:

> Teribus y teri odin
> Sons of heroes slain at Floadden
> Imitating Border bowmen
> Aye defend your rights and Common.

I wish to God they could find a better penultimate line, but there it is. Then the audience filed out and the Riding was proclaimed from the balcony.

I went with the Provost — a fellow of infinite jest, of most excellent fancy — an exciseman — to the Callants' Club, where we had more songs and speeches and quite a lot of whisky. All the songs were home-made and rather Victorian. There was only one really good one, about four-hundred horsemen. And another called RING THE BELL, KINLEY.

Then we went to a party at the Provost's house.

I got to bed at five (between four and five we had about a dozen of champagne with the Jubilee Cornet who carried the flag in 1900). I told the porter to waken me at 6.30, as I had to attend the Provost's breakfast at 7.30. At 7.45 the Housekeeper woke me to say, 'The police are wanting ye.' I said, 'I've done nothing. Tell them to go to Hell', and suddenly realised that I was already late for breakfast. I jumped up, shaved, and was round before eight. Ham and eggs, whisky, tea and some more speeches.

I told them that the only thing I had missed in their heathen rites was a human sacrifice; but that I was beginning to see that there might be one after all.

We then went in procession round the town and up a long, steep hill, the band playing in front like to bust themselves. At the top of the hill we stopped and watched the Cornet and his hundred followers coming up the road at full gallop. Hard on the beasts but very nice.

Into the cars again and up to the hill farm where we had curds and cream and rum and milk in a big hut to more speeches and songs.

Then at the racecourse, more whisky in the Provost's tent, a gallop round the course by the Cornet, and the planting of the flag.

I met K. Elliot on the course and went back to Harwood with her for lunch. Walter was in Nigeria. After lunch, I slept like a log till five. We drove back to Hawick to the Provost's and at six o'clock were at the Cornet's Dinner in the Crown Hotel. That went on — better speaking than I have ever heard anywhere — till ten. Then there were two Balls.

I didn't see a parson and only one drunk man all the time I was there. The drunk man was a visitor from Glasgow.

I enjoyed it. It was very elegant — as good as the THREE ESTATES. I thought I'd tell you.

It was a piece of natural religion, probably better and more sanitary than the A.D. variety. Indeed, God was hardly mentioned, except when He was asked — once, I think — to save the King.

Dramatic Works

Listed below are the principal dramatic works of James Bridie. Where plays had pre-London runs, the corrupt usage of giving the London opening as the First Performance has been adopted.

The Sunlight Sonata. 20th March 1928: The Scottish National Players at the Lyric Theatre, Glasgow: dir. Tyrone Guthrie.

The Switchback. 9th March 1929: Birmingham Repertory Theatre: dir. H. K. Ayliff.

What It Is To Be Young. 2nd November 1929: Birmingham Repertory Theatre: dir. H. K. Ayliff.

The Anatomist. 3rd July 1930: The Masque Theatre Company at the Royal Lyceum Theatre, Edinburgh: dir. Claud Gurney.

The Girl Who Did Not Want To Go To Kuala Lumpur. 12th November 1930: The Scottish National Players at the Lyric Theatre, Glasgow: dir. Elliot Mason.

Tobias and the Angel. 20th November 1930: The Festival Theatre, Cambridge: dir. Evan John, with Tyrone Guthrie as the Angel.

The Dancing Bear. 24th February 1931: The Scottish National Players at the Lyric Theatre, Glasgow: dir. W. G. Fay.

Jonah and the Whale. 12th December 1932: Westminster Theatre: dir. Henry Oscar, with Edward Chapman as Jonah.

A Sleeping Clergyman. 29th July 1933: Malvern Festival Theatre: dir. H. K. Ayliff, with Robert Donat and Dorice Fordred.

Marriage Is No Joke. 6th February 1934: Globe Theatre: dir. H. K. Ayliff, with Ralph Richardson and Sophie Stewart.

Colonel Wotherspoon. 23rd March 1934: The Scottish National Players at the Lyric Theatre, Glasgow: dir. Andrew Stewart.

Mary Read. 21st November 1934: His Majesty's Theatre: dir. Tyrone Guthrie, with Flora Robson and Robert Donat.

The Black Eye. 11th October 1935: Shaftesbury Theatre: dir. H. K. Ayliff, with Stephen Haggard.

Storm in a Teacup. 5th February 1936: Royalty Theatre: dir. W. G. Fay, with Sara Algood and Roger Livesey.

Susannah and the Elders. 31st October 1937: Duke of York's Theatre: dir. H. K. Ayliff, with Joan White.

The King of Nowhere. 15th March 1938: The Old Vic: dir. Esme Church, with Laurence Olivier, Vivienne Bennett and Alexander Knox.

Babes in the Wood. 18th June 1938: Embassy Theatre: dir. Dennis Arundell, with Alexander Knox and Angela Baddeley.

The Last Trump. 5th August 1938: Malvern Festival Theatre: dir. H. K. Ayliff, with Frank Pettingel.

The Golden Legend of Shults. 25th July 1939: Perth Theatre: dir. Norman MacDermott, with James Gibson.

What Say They? 7th August 1939: Malvern Festival Theatre: dir. H. K. Ayliff, with Yvonne Arnaud and Alastair Sim.

The Dragon and the Dove. 14th September 1942: Lyric Theatre, Glasgow: dir. E. Martin Browne.

Holy Isle. 8th December 1942: Arts Theatre Club: dir. Alastair Sim, with Alec Clunes.

Mr Bolfry. 3rd August 1943: Westminster Theatre: dir. Alastair Sim, with Alastair Sim, Raymond Lovell and Sophie Stewart.

It Depends What You Mean. 11th October 1944: Westminster Theatre: dir. Alastair Sim, with Alastair Sim, Angela Baddeley and Wilfred Hyde-Whyte.

The Forrigan Reel. 25th December 1944: Glasgow Citizens' Theatre: dir. Eric Capon, with Duncan Macrae, Molly Urquhart and James Gibson.

Lancelot. 4th November 1945: Glasgow Citizens' Theatre: dir. Matthew Forsyth, with Michael Golden.

The Pyrates' Den. 18th December 1945: Glasgow Citizens' Theatre (Pantomime).

John Knox. 18th August 1947: Glasgow Citizens' Theatre: dir. John Casson, with John Laurie and Mary McAlpine.

Dr Angelus. 30th July 1947: Phoenix Theatre: dir. Alastair Sim, with Alastair Sim and George Cole.

Gog and Magog. 1st December 1948: Arts Theatre Club: dir. Alec Clunes, with Alec Clunes, Richard Wordsworth and James Hayter.

Daphne Laureola. 23rd March 1949: Wyndham's Theatre: dir. Murray Macdonald, with Edith Evans and Peter Finch.

Mr Gillie. 13th February 1950: Garrick Theatre: dir. Alastair Sim, with Alastair Sim, Sophie Stewart and George Cole.

The Queen's Comedy. 21st August 1950: Glasgow Citizens' Theatre Company at the Royal Lyceum Theatre, Edinburgh (Edinburgh Festival): dir. Tyrone Guthrie and John Casson, with Sonia Dresdel and Walter Fitzgerald.

The Baikie Charivari. 6th October 1952: Glasgow Citizens' Theatre: dir. Peter Potter, with Donald Eccles and Ursula Jeans.

Meeting At Night. 17th May 1954: Glasgow Citizens' Theatre: dir. Michael Langham, with Duncan Macrae and Madeleine Christie.